ets of
cting
rship
rning
mor

eter M. Jonas

ScarecrowEducation
Lanham, Maryland • Toronto • Oxford
2004

Published in the United States of America
by ScarecrowEducation
An imprint of The Rowman & Littlefield Publishing Group, Inc.
4501 Forbes Boulevard, Suite 200, Lanham, Maryland 20706
www.scaroweducation.com

PO Box 317
Oxford
OX2 9RU, UK

British Library Cataloguing in Publication Information Available

Library of Congress Cataloging-in-Publication Data

Jonas, Peter M.
    Secrets of connecting leadership and learning with humor / Peter M. Jonas.
      p. cm.
    Includes bibliographical references and index.
    ISBN 1-57886-151-9 (pbk. : alk. paper)
    1. Humor in education.   2. Educational leadership.   3. College teaching.
   I. Title.
    LB2326.J66 2004
   371.3—dc22

                                 2004003440

∞™ The paper used in this publication meets the minimum requirements of
American National Standard for Information Sciences—Permanence of Paper
for Printed Library Materials, ANSI/NISO Z39.48-1992.
Manufactured in the United States of America.

To:

Nancy, who politely explained why I was not funny, but laughed at my jokes anyway.

Katie, who laughs at everything because she is so nice and does not want to hurt my feelings.

Mel, who pretends not to laugh, but is cracking up deep down inside.

Kevin, who laughs at everything because this is just his personality.

Contents

Figures

Acknowledgments

This work is dedicated to everyone who has ever told a joke and heard that awful silence that follows instead of laughter. Therefore, there was a great deal of inspiration from everyone who tried and failed, from students who may not have laughed but let me try again, and to the other students who are now getting a high grade because they did laugh.

I always tell my students to start with the general and work to the specific, so here we go. Jack and Nancy Jonas must have instilled a sense of humor, inquiry, compassion, and analysis that has allowed me to grow over the years. They both must have had a great sense of humor to put up with five kids. Sara, Jack, Tim, and Dan should be commended for not killing me as we were growing up. They probably had ever right to do it. My "family" of friends and colleagues at Cardinal Stritch University certainly created an atmosphere of creativity, dedication, the pursuit of knowledge, and the capacity to learn. The College of Education is truly a learning community that allows "research on humor" to be labeled as true scholarship. They laugh at me and with me—I think. Of course, I have to mention the doctoral students, who had to suffer through all those long weekends of teaching research, technology, and humor. Thanks for all the material.

Roger Aalderks has to receive special mention for doing all of the dirty work on the research. He not only has a great work ethic, but he is fun to be around. Mike, thanks for handouts, videos, and everything else. You are not getting them back. Thanks to Scott and Joel from BVK, and my good friends Don and Alex, who supplied some of the more interesting material to the research. And thanks to all of the guys (and ladies) who I play basketball with every week; you don't know how much you inspired me over the years. However, you have not done anything to help with my jump shot.

How to Use This Book

Secrets of Connecting Leadership and Learning with Humor is a research-based book that explores how humor is connected to the brain and can be used to enhance learning and leadership. The book attempts to use research to build a theoretical foundation for these concepts and then provide practical components for connecting leadership, learning, and humor.

Individuals need to understand the theoretical nature of leadership before they can put it into practice on a daily basis. The same is true for humor. The main theme of the book is that the proper use of humor will not only increase learning comprehension but that it can also be used as a strong tool for leaders to enhance their effectiveness. Throughout the text, I have interjected humorous jokes, stories, puns, expressions, and so forth in order to show examples of the theory or context and to provide the reader with material that can be used in leadership situations or in the classroom. The jokes and stories can be learned, put in a database, or copied for use as overheads. Moreover, each chapter contains information that is fun to read as well as practical examples of how to integrate humor into leadership activities and the classroom.

1

Introduction to Humor or Make Me Laugh

You do not stop laughing because you grow old, you grow old because you stop laughing.

Secrets of Connecting Leadership and Learning with Humor is not an attempt to establish the true meaning and nature of leadership. James Mac-Gregor Burns (1978), one of the leading authorities on the subject, wrote that leadership is one of the most examined and least understood phenomena in the world. Thousands of empirical investigations on leadership have been completed over the past seventy-five years, but no clear and indisputable understanding exists as to what distinguishes leaders from non-leaders (Bennis and Nanus 1985). This book is an attempt to define humor, explore the main characteristics of leadership and learning, and then provide practical ways to integrate them all—and have some fun in the process. This does not mean that every leader needs to become another Carrot Top—thank goodness. Humor is a natural, daily activity for teachers and leaders to enhance their effectiveness. In reality, teachers *are* leaders, so the suggestions offered throughout the text focus on learning, teaching, and leadership, which overlap in a multiplicity of areas.

This study does not attempt to present the ultimate meaning of leadership or the components of learning; others have been there, done that, and bought the T-shirt. The key to transforming yourself into a leader takes knowing what leadership is, understanding basic concepts of learning, and providing a service to others—that is, putting it into practice. This study presents research on humor to establish a theoretical foundation, along with practical examples of integrating humor, leadership, and learning. You will notice that numerous stories, jokes, puns, and so forth are sprinkled throughout the text. This is done not only to demonstrate in a practical fashion of how to use humor but also to demonstrate that the reader can use the material in many situations. The longest journey does not start with the first step, it starts with www.mapquest.com. By the way, if you are still walking, you should buy a car instead of this book.

DEFINITIONS OF HUMOR

The first step in the process is to define humor. Not that anyone really knows how to do this, but it sounds like that should be done in a book like this. In 1970, Davis and Farina found humor to be "a whole composite of different behaviors rather than a single one, and any explanation which attempts to explain them equally would appear to be doomed to do so by explaining them marginally" (175). Many others have attempted to define humor by using examples or descriptors, or even through philosophy, like Sorrell stating "laughter lifts man above his animalistic state, sets him free, and gives his spirituality another dimension" (11). Still others use basic characteristics of humor in their definitions, such as social, cognitive, physiological, or psychological aspects. Ultimately, humor is defined as "a verbal or nonverbal activity eliciting a positive cognitive or affective response from listeners." Another key element is that humor must be connected to context in order to be truly funny (Meyer 1990). This means that humor can include the spoken word, jokes, puns, silly exercises, handouts, overheads, unusual or physical activities, stories, or even pithy sayings.

Humor is somewhat elusive partially because it changes over time with each new generation. Some things are timeless, but have you ever heard a joke on TV from a show twenty years old and it just was not funny? For example, listening to Ralph Cramdon threaten to hit Alice by saying "Pow, zoom, to the moon" is not as funny today as it was years ago because of the rising concern in domestic abuse. Humor changes as new information is discovered and each generation develops its own nuances within the culture. Today, we think it is funny to suggest that the Ethernet is something used to catch the etherbunny.

There are many theories about "change" in history, but Plato argued that what people think is real and permanent in life is not. He explained that most individuals think inanimate objects like tables, chairs, or desks are real. However, this is not true because in a hundred years these items will no longer exist. The ideas or concepts of a table, chair, or desk are real because they will be the same after one hundred years. Similarly, the idea of humor is much more real than what is humorous. Humor is forever, but what we find humorous changes.

> The root of the English word "humor" is the Latin *umor,* meaning "liquid, fluid." Perhaps, humor is something that flows within us and courses through us with the ability to refresh perspective, heal attitudes, and balance our equilibrium. The *American Heritage Dictionary* helpfully offers "a capacity to appreciate or understand" as a designation for a sense of humor. That may be the most helpful clue of all. (Donnelly 1992)

Humor not only involves the fluids of the body but it also has to do with connections to the brain, the heart, the soul, and spirit of individuals, as well as the social, spiritual, emotional, and relational aspects of people, which partially explains the expression "growing weak with laughter." It is a state of mind that can create balance in one's life with body, mind, and soul.

Humor is not something to laugh at. Similar to leadership, the definitions and characteristics of humor have been the subject of many academic arguments. Of course, academicians always resort to complex theoretical structures when explaining even the most basic human activity—for example, laughing.

> The specific theory [of humor]-building procedures utilized a combination of heuristic and rounded theory methodologies that identified and examined variables that cause psycho physiological arousal. Three sources of arousal were found: 1) personality variables involving certain traits, states, and habits; 2) social contexts such as the presence of another person, social situations, and sociocultural norms; 3) stimulus (joke) properties including salient content, joke structure, and personal values. As several of these variables combine, arousal increases to a moderate intensity, then drops abruptly with the punch line or the conclusion of an amusing situation. (Glueck 2001, iv–vi)

Now I do not claim to be an expert in this area—well, actually I do because I am writing this book—but this theory appears to be a little too academic. However, parts of it are useful. (You may have heard the expression that "All models are wrong, but some of them are useful"? Same concept here.) Now if this is what it takes to laugh, it just may not be worth the effort. By the way, this is an example of irony, using a less-than-funny quote to help define humor. Moreover, I am using a quote from the dissertation abstract; after all, you don't expect me to read the entire dissertation, do you? They are typically boring, except as noted.

One of the best ways to understand humor is through examples, and where better to look for humorous examples of educational research than dissertations? The dissertation typically carries high academic standards, and the use of humor in such an important entity shows how useful it can be. Some of the more unusual (and humorous) dissertation titles and entries are listed below, and as Dave Barry would write, "I am not making this up." This just goes to demonstrate that humor, research, and leadership can be connected. For example, did you know that actor/comedian Bill Cosby received an EdD from the University of Massachusetts at Amherst in 1977 for *An Integration of Visual Media via "Fat Albert and the Cosby Kids" into the Elementary School Curriculum as a Teaching Aid and Vehicle to Achieve Increased Learning* (Creguer 1991, 4). Some of the best titles of dissertations come from the masses. Here are a few of the more interesting works of research with a basis for humor. (Again, I am not making these up.)

- *Classification of Drinking Styles Using the Topographical Components of Beer Drinking*
- *Garage Sales as Practice*
- *Things That Are Good and Things That Are Chocolate: A Cultural Model of Weight Control as Morality*
- *There's No Excuse for Chocolate Pizza* (Creguer 1991, 4–5)

So, as you can see, humor finds its way into even the most academically oriented research. But some of the best humor is found in the dedications of dissertations. For example, one graduate student wrote: "I wish to thank my wife and daughter for the pants. I wanted a camera, but the pants will be fine" (Creguer 1991, 46). However, the best dedication comes from a long-winded and sarcastic graduate student who wrote:

If I had a dime for every time my wife threatened to divorce me during the past three years, I would be wealthy and not have to take a postdoctoral position which will only make me a little less poor and will keep me away from home and in the lab even more than graduate school and all because my committee read this manuscript and said that the only alternative to signing the approval to this dissertation was to give me a job mowing the grass on campus but the Physical Plant would not hire me on account of they said I was over-educated and needed to improve my dexterity skills like picking my nose while driving a tractor-mower over poor defenseless squirrels that were eating the nuts they stole from the medical students' lunches on Tuesday afternoon following the Biochemistry quiz which they all did not pass and blamed on me because they said a tutor was supposed to come with a 30-day money-back guarantee and I am supposed to thank someone for all of this?!!! (Creguer 1991, 46)

Clearly these are practical examples of using humor as a stress reliever, but humor is more than the verbal or nonverbal activity eliciting a positive cognitive or affective response from listeners; humor must also include five specific variables.

VARIABLES IN HUMOR

With any definition, numerous circumstances or variables come into play. The following variables will be used in order to add more specificity to the definition of humor: 1) associated with the social context of the situation, 2) the cognitive challenge, 3) the novelty, 4) its timing, and 5) the degree of detachment (Coleman 1992, 270–271).

Variable #1

Social context—the audience must be informed or knowledgeable about the social context of the joke and they must be able to relate to it. Example: How many times have you heard a speaker tell a story at the start of a long speech or presentation? The joke may be funny but, more times than not, it does not relate to the subject or have any social context. In 2000, the keynote speaker, who will be called *Mr. X* to protect the guilty, at a national conference talked about the importance of institutional researchers in the world today. The speaker started the keynote with the following joke.

A man was walking in the airport carrying two large suitcases. He stopped for a moment, put down the suitcases, pressed his watch, and started talking to his secretary. He said that he would be at the office in a few minutes and was faxing over some documents. He pressed another button on the watch to fax the information. A woman nearby was amazed at this technology. Imagine being able to have a watch, telephone, and fax machine on your wrist. The woman offered the man $2,000 for the watch but he refused. She then offered $5,000 and he reluctantly agreed. She took the watch and started to walk away when the man lifted up the two suitcases and said, "Wait a minute! Don't you want the batteries?"

The keynote committed the mortal sin of telling one bad joke to start the speech and then never adding any more humor while speaking for one and one-half hours on multiple linear regressions and factor analysis—which is probably a bigger joke than the one at the start of the speech. Nevertheless, the joke had no connection or context to the theme of the speech. Humor has specific methods to be used and it can sometimes hurt a good speaker or leader as much as it can help. Humor is meant to be used by professionals—so kids, don't try this at home.

Earlier in his career, Steve Martin provided a great example of using the appropriate social context in humor when he tells the joke about the plumber who completes a very detailed and delicate job. In the joke, Martin uses exaggerated and inaccurate "plumber" terminology as he explains how the professional had to use the six-sided hexagonal frosberg wrench to tighten the longesbate screws on a sink tripod socket. The punch line comes when the other plumber then says, "I thought you said sprocket, not socket." No one laughs, so Steve then says, "This is the plumbers convention, isn't it?" The first rule of thumb for using humor is to "know your audience." (Do you know where "rule of thumb" comes from? Back in the sixteenth century it was actually acceptable for a man to beat his wife with an object, provided the object was smaller than the thickness of his thumb, hence the phrase, "rule of thumb.")

Variable #2

Cognitive challenge—humor has to challenge the audience. You cannot offer a third-grade-level joke to a college professor. (Well, actually, maybe you can. "If you see a college professor hanging by one hand from a tree, how do you get him down? Wave to him." Be honest, you laughed! I have the license to tell this joke because I am a college professor and typically hang around in trees.)

A real-life example occurred when a prominent American company fired its CEO after nine months, saying he lacked "intellectual leadership." He received a $26-million severance package. Perhaps it is not the CEO who lacked intellectual leadership or had a "cognitive challenge."

Variable #2 is actually quite difficult to gauge because you must be able to challenge the audience without insulting them or losing them in the process. Leaders need to use humor in a seamless fashion so that it becomes part of their character, is not forced, and is on the same level as the rest of the information. Your audience needs to be able to understand the joke without struggling too hard or your message is lost.

Variable #3

Novelty—if something is unique or out of the ordinary, then there could be a great possibility for humor. Leaders need to change. The world of leadership today is fraught with constant change, progression, and complexity. Some of the most insightful leaders are not only accepting of change but they continuously transform themselves as they serve as change-agents. Consequently, leaders will more often than not prove to be the model of consistency in order to add stability to the change process. However, the integration of novelty into the daily grind helps sell the message of change and makes the leader more human, that is, to be seen as part of the group. Remember, the only difference between a rut and a grave is the dimensions.

For example, in 1996, I was one of five members of a panel discussing the effect of assessment on education. Hundreds of individuals from a national business organization listened to the panel group of "experts." I was the second person to speak. The main point of the presentation was that very few faculty seem to like assessment. It is similar to the time a top aide of President Reagan asked, "Ron, why is it that people take an immediate dislike to me?" President Reagan supposedly answered, "John, because it simply saves time." Most faculty feel the same way about assessment: they hate it before they get to know it—and after they learn about the details, they probably hate it even more.

In the presentation, I explained that with assessment it is all a matter of attitude, or how you approach the topic. I offered this analogy:

> There is a story about one of the first management consultants who walked around a stone quarry interviewing workers. He stopped by one worker who was grumbling and cursing under his breath and the consultant asked him what he was doing. The response was sharp and curt, "What the heck does it look like I'm doing? I'm cutting rocks." The consultant walked away hurriedly and approached another individual who was working quietly but steadily. He asked what he was doing. "I'm cutting stones for building and I'm busy!" Finally, the consultant spotted a worker who was whistling cheerfully as he chiseled away. When asked the same question, this worker replied, "I'm building a cathedral." The moral of the story is that cathedral builders make the best employees, and it's all in the way you look at things.

Once you get some individuals to take the right attitude on assessment, they will be models for the entire faculty. However, this may not always be the key to success. One time I was at a seminar in Atlanta, Georgia, and was introduced as a model husband, a model citizen, and a model faculty. I was very honored until I looked up the definition of "model" in the dictionary and it said "a small imitation of the real thing."

Now you do not have to attend any of my presentations on assessment, because you got the entire speech right here. After the thundering and almost deafening applause from the audience, I took my place back on the panel. (I may be slightly exaggerating here, but it fits the story line.) The reason for any success of the presentation was the connection of the jokes to each of the three main points. The audience might not always remember the details of the speech but they remember the jokes and associate them with the message. The moral of the story is to be prepared, be unique, and then be seated.

Variable #4

Timing—timing is everything in comedy, and this is especially true in connecting humor to leadership. Jean Lipman-Blumen writes in *The Connective Edge* (1996) that there are three sets or behaviors of leaders: direct, relational, and instrumental. Each set has three separate styles identified for leaders. Lipman-Blumen found that leaders tend to find a small

number of styles that they are comfortable with and then rely on these be
haviors. However, the truly great leaders are able to use the appropriate
behavior out of the nine different styles in the appropriate circumstances.
Using different behavioral sets involves being flexible enough to try different styles of leadership, and using the ability to analyze a situation
through reflection. Lipman-Blumen's theory is very similar to the concept
of integrating humor into leadership: Timing is everything. Leaders need
to have a bag of tricks (or different styles) to use when appropriate. The
key is being able to determine the most appropriate form of humor at the
right time. Take the jokes, stories, puns, or activities in the book and keep
them in a database or on note cards to use later. Be sure to keep notes on
the responses to the jokes. It is important to track the reactions of others
to your humor to see what works in what particular situation.

An example of how important timing is came in 1995, while I was serving as the keynote to a group of college and university educators. This was
a typical conference, just like one that you might have attended hundreds
of times. You prepare the speech, check the facts, and be sure you have a
solid point. Because the topic dealt mainly with technology, I started the
presentation with the following observation:

> A woman married to a systems analyst wanted to get a divorce. When she
> appeared in court, the judge asked why she wanted a divorce after ten years
> of marriage. The woman replied that her husband was a technology systems
> analyst and was useless in the bedroom (and probably elsewhere, too, but
> we are not going to get into that). She said that all he does is sit on the side
> of the bed and say how good sex will be.

This may not be the funniest joke in the world but it related directly to
the main point of the speech—that technology systems analysts are known
more for talking than doing. Nevertheless, you could hear a pin drop for
the rest of the presentation. I realize not everyone can be Dennis Miller (or
Don Rickles if you are from a slightly older crowd), but some of the jokes
were good, at least worth a giggle if nothing else. But after forty-five minutes of speaking, there was still not a peep from the audience. Why? Anyway, I received a polite applause at the conclusion of the speech, and I
slithered to my seat and sat down next to a friend. Leaning over to Mar-
lene, I asked, "What the heck just happened here with the speech?" Mar-
lene smiled and said that it was bad timing on my part. Recently, one of the

vocal leaders in the organization had just been caught cheating on his wife and the rumors were flying all around the conference about the impending divorce. And of course, he was an technology ststems expert. My timing could not have been worse. I was never invited back to this convention—can't imagine why. Remember, if you are digging yourself a hole, the least you can do is stop shoveling.

Variable #5

Degree of detachment is present—people are more than willing to laugh at things that do not touch too close to home or to things that we are sensitive about. We laugh more when we are not part of the punch line. How many Notre Dame alumni does it take to change a light bulb? Thousands, one to change the light bulb and the rest to reminisce about the old bulb. Now, this joke is funnier to a Marquette University graduate than a Notre Dame alumnus. (I just love the joke—would you like to know where I graduated?) Of course, you can simply reverse this joke and ask how many Marquette alumni does it take to screw in a light bulb?

Leaders tend to be considered role models for their organizations or community and consequently are placed under a microscope more than most people. It is even more important to be careful about what, when, and how leaders say and do things because they could very easily be misconstrued. A simple joke about work habits can be blown out of proportion and create ill feelings because of a misperceived connection to the comment. Therefore, the degree of detachment is a variable that must be addressed when leaders use humor. I know a dean who would sometimes joke with those of his staff who came into work late. He would say, "It's nice to see you found the way into the office." The staff never thought it was a funny comment and usually resented the implication.

At another university, I was brought in to talk about technology in education. I was feeling exceptionally philosophical and told the tale of Prometheus. This story takes place at the time when mortals were being created. The Titan Epimetheus and his brother Prometheus were given the task of providing living creatures with a means of protection. Epimetheus gave the slow tortoise a hard shell so he would be protected from attack and the tasty rabbit was given good eyesight and great speed. Epimetheus was so generous that when it came time to take care of mankind, nothing was left to give. Mankind had fair eyesight, but not nearly as good as that of his predators. He was given the capacity to run, but not very fast. Humans were ill prepared for life on the Earth, and this suited Zeus just fine. Prometheus felt that mankind needed a special gift and in order to assist these special beings he flew to the heavens and stole fire, or technology, from Zeus as a present for humankind.

I equated the gift of fire to technology and then explained that eventually Epimetheus married Pandora. Pandora found a jar containing all the spites of mankind that Prometheus had hidden away—old age, sickness, labor, insanity, vice, and passion. Upon opening the jar, all the vices escaped. Just as technology can be filled with many of the negatives if handled inappropriately, it is all in the use and attitude.

Why did I go the historical and academic route with the speech? Remember that academicians want to be challenged intellectually, and will pretend to get a joke even if they don't understand it, especially if they do not have tenure. However, people do not want to be offended by the humor. Two days earlier, I had been speaking at a different college. Instead of using the good old Prometheus and Pandora example, I had equated technology with alcoholism and how both can be addictions. I thought that this was a particularly poignant point, but one person in the audience took exception to the analogy by telling me after the speech that alcoholism was not funny. This individual obviously had little or no detachment to the subject, so in order not to offend anyone else I changed the context of the story.

Thus, the definition of humor has several variables. It can hit different people in different ways, depending on the circumstances. Leaders cannot just use humor and expect the desired outcome to materialize without planning. Like many characteristics of leadership, humor needs to be used in the appropriate way, and in the appropriate setting. Remember, even if you are on the right track, you get run over if you are just sitting there.

Here is a generic process on how to develop your own humor for teaching or leadership situations.

1. Brainstorm the main topic area that you need to discuss.
2. Brainstorm ideas and facts about the topic.
3. Then write observations on the facts.
4. It is easier to write jokes about the real-life observations that you have experienced.

5. Develop humor along with the observations. One common technique is to use similes, comparisons, and contrasts with the observations. For example, contrasting two incongruent ideas is almost always funny.
6. Look for observations that are popular or "in" with the crowd.
7. Paint a picture for the audience.
8. Refine, refine, and refine the joke (Adult Learning Program 2001)

PRACTICAL POINTS TO PONDER

Here are fifteen tips on how to define and develop humor for leaders and teachers.

1. Field-test the material before using it. You may want to find a colleague, friend, or companion to try your jokes on. Find someone in your own field to work with.
2. Use jokes that are practical. Try to think of common experiences or things that your students or colleagues consider an annoyance. Everyone loves to know they are not alone in their complaints.
3. Always relate the jokes to the audience. This means that you need to do some homework before using humor. What age are your students or staff? What are they talking about or complaining about? Talk with students ahead of time to find out what is on their minds. Be sure to read the room. If people are not paying attention, notice this fact and move on to something else. This means that you should know your audience and its culture.
4. Less is more with a joke. You should set up the joke appropriately, get into the story, tell the punch line, and get out.
5. Be enthusiastic in what you do. The topic and jokes must come from the heart because the audience can tell if you are not sincere about the subject matter. Remember, you must love what you do but do not show fear. Students or colleagues can be like sharks and will attack the fearful. Just like the line in the *Santa Claus 2* movie: "Seeing is not believing; believing is seeing."
6. Converse with the your students and staff. Joke about the things you know and things that the people know so they can take ownership of the information.

7. It is easy to be funny, but you must ask yourself: Can the audience take notes from the speech? After all, the point of using humor is to be a better leader or teacher. If the audience cannot take notes from your speech, than you have a content problem.

8. Body language is crucial. People will be watching your eye movement, body language, and so on—so you need to make your body work for you when using humor.

9. Be original with jokes and do not use ones used a hundred times before—as I am doing in this book.

10. Practice jokes ahead of time and choose your words carefully. Be detailed when telling a story. The more details you can add, the more believable it will be. For example, use the word *mackerel* instead of the word *fish*. Some words and phrases are just funny in their nature. For example, scenes repeated from funny movies like *Caddyshack* are good foundations for jokes.

11. In order to get good at integrating humor into class or presentations, you need to practice, practice, practice. Do not expect to be excellent the first time through. Your comfort level will rise the more times you try with the humor.

12. Keep a notebook with you at all times to write down funny comments, observations, and so forth that you can use.

13. Like anything, there is a learning curve in using humor. Read books on the topic of humor and always have a thesaurus, rhyming dictionary, book of quotes, and clichés at hand. There are even good books (but not as good as this one) on funny handouts, how to be funny at the podium, and similar topics. In fact, every organization, group of kids, and school has its own clichés used on a daily basis. Learn to speak the language in order to include it in the humor.

14. In humor, there is a rule of threes. Whenever you use a list in your humor, you should include three items. The first two items should be normal, with the last one that being the unexpected and funny item. For example, there are three things that you need to know about homework: 1) it helps students learn the material, 2) practice makes perfect, and 3) parents appreciate homework so they can finally get the TV.

15. Trust the process and "be the joke" (from the movie *Caddyshack*).

2

Purposes of Humor or
Humor Is No Laughing Matter

PURPOSES OF HUMOR

One of the common characteristics of leaders is that they are prepared and have a vision. Quality teachers have detailed lesson plans, quality leaders have strategic plans, and both have designed purposes for what they do. Using humor is no different; there must be a purpose to the madness. Typically, the research identifies four main reasons for using humor in leadership endeavors: 1) contrasting incongruent ideas, 2) providing a feeling of superiority over others, 3) releasing strain and tension, and 4) coping with an ambiguous audience or environment (Hudson 1979).

Contrasting Incongruent Ideas

Humans, and the human brain, like continuity and certainty. Contrasting incongruent ideas or making fun of concepts that do not make sense are prime purposes for using humor. People do not want to be the only ones who do not understand a concept, process, or system. It is more reassuring to be part of a group, even if that group is in the dark. In addition, by putting the incongruity on the table, it can be better analyzed. Bloom's taxonomy notes that analysis and synthesis are the highest forms of learning. Therefore, humor used for contrasting incongruent ideas can lead to a higher form of learning. Take the example of the faculty member, academic dean, and vice president all convicted of a serious crime

15

and punished to die by the guillotine. (This is a true story, if you believe my students.)

> When the faculty member was placed in the guillotine, she was asked if she would like to die with her head looking up or down. She chose to look down and when the blade was released, it did not fall. The executioner said that according to the rules of execution the faculty member must be spared. When the academic dean was placed in the guillotine he chose to be looking down also. Again the blade was released and did not fall. The academic dean was spared. When the vice president was placed in the guillotine, he chose to be looking up; always the forward-thinking person. At that point, the vice president said, "I think I see your problem—there's a loose bolt up there."

One of the most obvious uses of incongruent ideas is the oxymoron, and its first cousin, the pun. Both can be used as teaching techniques and by leaders to enhance certain leadership characteristics. By keeping a few of the puns or sayings memorized, you are able to call upon them in the correct setting.

> Evidence has been found that William Tell and his family were avid bowlers. However, all the league records were unfortunately destroyed in a fire. Thus we'll never know for whom the Tells bowled.

> A man rushed into the doctor's office and shouted, "Doctor! I think I'm shrinking!" The doctor calmly responded, "Now, settle down. You'll just have to be a little patient."

> Back in the 1800s the Tates Watch Company of Massachusetts wanted to produce other products and, since they already made the cases for pocket watches, decided to market compasses for the pioneers traveling West. It turned out that although their watches were of the finest quality, their compasses were so bad that people often ended up in Canada or Mexico rather than California. This, of course, is the origin of the expression, "He who has a Tates is lost!"

> A famous Viking explorer returned home from a voyage and found his name missing from the town register. His wife insisted on complaining to the local civic official who apologized profusely saying, "I must have taken Leif off my census."

When leaders come to the realization that members of an organization, school, or class do not understand a complex or incongruent situation, many of them go into the blame or CYA (cover your "behind") mode.

Consequently, this leads to a culture of "duck and cover." Whereas, if the incongruent concept becomes the focal point of a joke, the problem can be put on the table and discussed (sometimes in a humorous way), thereby enhancing communication and fostering a more productive culture.

Providing a Feeling of Superiority over Others

Providing a feeling of superiority over others can be based either on the in-adequacies of group or a deviation from the norm (Goldstein 1976). Many philosophers argue that the human condition is almost set automatically to take advantage of the differences in classes. Some leaders go so far as to say that this form of humor is almost a social reward (Hudson 1979). Of course, humor that is used to make the leader feel superior over someone can also be deemed derogatory to the group being ridiculed. Remember that the sword that is used to point can also be used to cut. Be careful using humor for a feeling of superiority because you can only step in a river once. (This is called *mixing metaphors* but I did get several pithy sayings in at once.)

Humor is somewhat like "the Force" in *Star Wars*; if used properly it can be a powerful tool for good to save the universe, but used inappropriately, it can be more like the Dark Side. Comedians will tell you that telling jokes to make the audience look superior (over you) is one way to win friends and influence people. For example, telling jokes that are self-ridiculing will make the audience feel superior to the teacher or leader. You can also con-sciously misuse terms or clichés, which will instill a sense of superiority in students and staff, and maybe even a feeling of empathy for you. Of course, you need a thick skin to make fun of yourself. Nevertheless, this may very well be one of the main components of servant-leadership.

> One day a man was driving down the road and he saw a beautiful farm. He stopped and complimented the farmer on the beautiful land and farm. "God must have been very generous when he gave you this land." The farmer replied, "Yes, God was generous but you should have seen the land when he had it all to himself."

Releasing Strain and Tension

Many times it is the surprise element of a story that facilitates humor. Consequently, this creates an emotional relief that makes the group more secure. People want to laugh and do not like to be in tension-filled situations. Humor can be used to break the ice, lessen tension, or open lines of communication in a delicate situation. Using humor to release strain or tension can be cathartic.

Some of the safest humorous interventions in stressful situations are "knock-knock" or "light bulb" jokes. Leaders and teachers can memorize various examples from both types of jokes and use them in the appropriate situation. Obviously, it is good to be able to match the joke with the situation, and "knock-knock" or "light bulb" jokes can easily be revised to fit the situation. For example, if you are discussing a delicate issue between teachers and administrators, try this one: How many administrators does it take to change a light bulb? One this year, two next year, and we budgeted for three the following year. How many faculty does it take to change a light bulb? Change? By taking a jab at both sides in the situation you are being an equal opportunity offender and not picking on just one group. Both sides should be able to laugh together.

With just a little reflection, the jokes can be altered easily to fit the proper situation. For example, how does a ballerina screw in a light bulb? She stands on a chair, holds the light bulb, and simply lets the world revolve around her. Simply take out the word "ballerina" and insert "principal" when discussing the leader of the school, or "teacher" when talking with an educational colleague.

Some of the best jokes can be completely unrelated to the topic being discussed. If used properly, the incongruent, nonrelated anecdote will may be just what is needed to relieve tension in a stressful situation. Moreover, there are some old, reliable subjects that almost everyone likes to criticize, like college athletics and psychologists, and therefore serve as easy targets for humor. How many college football players does it take to screw in a light bulb? Only one but he gets three credits for it. How many individuals under psychiatric care does it take to screw in a light bulb? One, but he really has to want to change.

What is the right joke for the right situation? There is no clear-cut answer to this question, but individuals need to be able to use various forms of humor. Some of the keys to matching humor to the situation are:

1. Always know your audience, class, or staff. Be able to talk the same language; know their likes, dislikes, and concerns in life.

2. Be sincere and knowledgeable with the content of your message and the humor associated with it. People are intelligent and can spot insincerity a mile away.

3. Do not talk down to your audience or use humor that is unrelated to the concerns of others. Dennis Miller learned this particular lesson quickly as commentator for *Monday Night Football*—he was "traded" for a different announcer.

4. Set up the joke, get in, and get out. In other words, relate the joke, saying, or humorous activity to the content of your message, and move on. Again, people are intelligent, they can understand your point, and they do not need something dwelled on for hours.

5. If the joke works for you, great. If the joke does not work for you, great. Do not give up on humor. Rome was not built in one day, and I am a history major so I should know. When using humor to enhance leadership skills, not everything will work. So what. Deal with it and move on, but do not stop trying. There is no crying in humor.

Coping with an Ambiguous Audience or Environment

When individuals are feeling out of place, they try coping in many different ways, by biting fingernails, eating, fiddling with their hair, or making jokes. Many people will use humor as a coping mechanism to feel more at ease in an uncomfortable situation.

One of the least effective uses of humor is when a chief executive officer, or other similar individual, starts off a speech, lecture, or meeting with a joke, and typically not a very good one. He or she then goes on to explain the financial nomenclature of the company's fourth quarter, without even attempting to make the joke relevant or using another story for the remainder of the speech. Using one bad joke within a situation does not help others to cope, or make you part of the group. It is too transparent and could even make the group resentful. But related stories are an excellent use of humor when coping with an ambiguous environment.

A man piloting a hot air balloon discovers he is hopelessly lost. He lowers the balloon to yell to a man on the ground, "Excuse me, can you tell me where I am?" The man below says, "Yes, you're in a hot air balloon, about thirty feet above this field." "You must work in information technology," says the balloonist. "Yes, I do," replies the man. "And how did you know that?" "Well," says the balloonist, "what you told me is technically correct, but of no use to anyone." The man below says, "You must work in management." "I do," replies the balloonist, "but how did you know?" "Well," says the man, "you don't know where you are, or where you're going, but you expect my immediate help. You're in the same position you were before we met, but now it's my fault!"

When it comes to ambiguous situations, there is a belief that leaders are there to comfort the afflicted and afflict the comfortable. Many times leaders need to give instructions and train others within an organization, which ultimately can be stressful or uncertain at times. Appropriately used, humor can ease the situation.

Humor can also be used to connect the environment with the leader. Bob (a friend of mine whom I told that I would put in a book—so now I have) is a talented educator who used to say when he took over as the vice president of a large university he was handed three envelopes by the president. He was told not to open them until he ran into trouble. Soon he needed some advice and after opening the first envelope, it read "Open lines of communication." He did this, but shortly needed to open the second envelope, which read "Form a committee." And finally, within a short time, he found himself in another desperate situation, so he opened the third envelope that read "Prepare three new envelopes."

It may be hard to believe, but I had another friend who became the president of a small, Midwestern, liberal arts college. (It is hard to believe I have two friends, not that he became a president.) Alex was warned that if he took the job, one of three things would happen: he would either get fired, get a divorce, or die. He took the job and was fired two years later—probably the lesser of the three evils. Alex realized he was in both a unique and ambiguous environment, and relied upon humor to help him through. He always had high standards and was always prepared (just like the Boy Scouts). He is one of those leaders who planned for everything, even the interjection of jokes at the appropriate time. His key to using humor was to look spontaneous and always be overprepared. Trust me, ill-timed humor can do more harm than you may realize.

You may be asking yourself, why did he get fired if Alex was so well prepared, humorous, organized, and such a quality leader? The answer is that he was placed in a very ambiguous situation. The moral of the story is that even the best leaders sometimes find themselves in circumstances that are beyond their control. Humor helps leaders, but it is really only a tool to achieve a certain end and is not a cure for everything that ails.

In the movie *Little Big Man*, the Native American grandfather, played by Chief Dan George, determines it is a good day to die. He makes his arrangements, calls for his buffalo robes, goes out onto the prairie, lies down, and waits. Time passes; it begins to rain. Another character mournfully comes to check on him and discovers Grandfather is still alive! Chief Dan George arises with great dignity, gathers his belongings, and says to his companion, "Sometimes the magic happens, sometimes it doesn't." It is the same with humor.

PRACTICAL POINTS TO PONDER

There are four main purposes for using humor: 1) contrasting incongruent ideas, 2) providing a feel of superiority over others, 3) releasing strain and tension, and 4) coping with an ambiguous audience or environment. Here are a few suggestions for integrating leadership, learning, and humor.

1. Lists are an excellent way of combing humor with content. David Letterman is the king of top ten lists, but that does not preclude others from using the concept. As a leader, if you are trying to solve a problem or brainstorm new ideas, allow participants to list humorous solutions. The humorous lists will not only help release tension, they may also lead to new ideas pertinent to the task at hand.
2. Carry around a supply of lists to be used at the right time.

    a. The thirty-five most interesting oxymorons—state worker, legally drunk, exact estimate.
    b. Interesting leadership books—*No One Is Listening until You Make a Mistake.*
    c. A list of *What I've Learned as a Leader . . . The Dysfunctional Version*—I've learned that it's not what you have in your life that counts but how much you have in your bank account. For more examples, see appendix A.

3. Overheads are a necessity for any leader. You may want to carry some standard overheads with you to class, speeches, or meetings. An assortment of jokes from cartoons like Dilbert are not only practical but funny. Concise sayings will also go a long way to make your point, and when you have them on an overheard ready to go, it makes a lasting impression—for example, Don't sweat the small stuff. Everything is the small stuff. For more examples, see appendix B.

4. Activities can be interesting, humorous, and informative. Learn three or four activities that you can do at the drop of a hat so that you can interject them at any time. Leaders can use the activities for any of the four purposes listed in this chapter. One such activity is to learn how to juggle. This is actually easier than you may think. By taking three scarves, you can demonstrate juggling to a group while making numerous analogies. For example, learning to juggle can be associated with juggling projects at school, practice makes perfect, or learning transpires best when theory and practice are integrated. Another activity could be card tricks. Once again, a good book on how to do card tricks can make you a magician within hours. Card tricks can also have many metaphors for valuable lessons, such as relating them to communication, deceitful activities of leaders, or making order out of chaos.

5. Have two or three group exercises memorized or written on a 3-×-5 card so you can refer to them at any time. (I actually have many exercises stored in a PDA.) Here are few examples, but there are countless books on resourceful and entertaining activities, such as *Playing Along* (1997) by Izzy Gesell or *A Handbook of Interactive Exercises for Groups* (1999) by Barlow, Blythe, and Edmonds.

   a. Tape a piece of paper on everyone's back with a joke written on it. Put the punch line on someone else's back. Do this for several jokes and have the people walk around reading each other's back to see where the joke fits the punch line.

   b. Divide the group into three to five participants. Hold up several ordinary objects, such as a pen, chalk, glasses, and so forth. Make the group find the most original, the most useless, and the funniest use for each of the objects. The idea is to have fun with the exercise, while promoting teamwork and creativity.

6. Put together a sheet of paper with random clip art pieces and ask individuals to select one picture to help represent how they are feeling. You can either use clip art from any software program or go to the font of Wingdings to select an even broader range of pictures. (You may need to enlarge the font size for Wingdings.) For example, ☺ ❀ 📖 ✓ ❑.

3

What Is Leadership? Or, He Ain't Heavy, He's (She's) My Leader

There is an age-old argument about whether leaders are born or made. This debate has gone on for some time, but the reality is that leadership can be developed—it is not a born trait. Leadership can be learned, if for no other reason than because I said so. (Using similar logic, I will make the same argument for humor being a result of nurturing, not nature.) In fact, the environment that we are nurtured in has a remarkable impact on our learning, behavior, values, and humor. Infants are born with billions and billions of neural connections and the environment has a direct affect on further development. In other words, the development of leadership is connected to the nurturing (teaching/learning) environment of the individual. Again, the same is true for the nurturing of humor. You are not a "born leader" or a "born humorist"; these are traits learned through your environment and the neurological developments of the brain.

The main function of the brain is to keep you alive by storing information vital to survival and getting rid of useless information. Interestingly, the brain weighs approximately three pounds and uses ten times more oxygen than your lungs, which is 25 percent of all energy produced by the body. Your brain works automatically, storing survival information in one of several different types of memory. The key is to get your brain to store the necessary information that will enhance leadership, learning, and humor. The process is the same for any of the three topics.

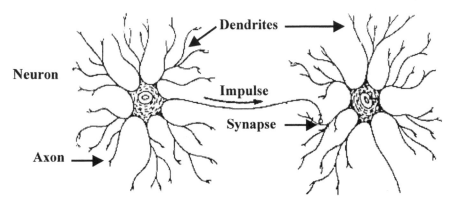

Figure 3.1. Chemical Reactions through Synapse

The brain is comprised of neurons (brain cells) with dendrites (tentacles of communication) that send impulses through chemical reactions through the synapses (gaps between dendrites). The brain is a complex organ, so in order to assist the learning process, the more connections that can be made to previous knowledge, the more efficient the learning process. Consequently, through occurrences that happen every day, the synapses in the brain make the connections that enhance leadership ability through the mistakes you make over time and the learning that occurs.

All sensory input passes through the amygdala, which is the security part of the brain and which also determines emotional responses. It is the survival part of the brain, which constantly asks the question: "Do I eat it, does it eat me, or do I mate with it?" The bottom line is that the brain needs to understand the content of the information to be learned, it must be deemed important, and then it has to be connected to some other relevant information already stored in memory. Because humor is a universal language, the concept is already stored in the working memory of most people, so leadership activities tied to humor can be connected in the brain and thereby more easily stored in memory.

We do know that leadership is more a factor of being nurtured than being part of nature, but the latter certainly plays a role.

Once upon a time there was a frog and scorpion. The scorpion approached the frog and asked for a ride across a pond. The frog said, "No, because you will sting me and we will drown." The scorpion responded, "No, I won't because I need you. I have to get across the pond and cannot swim. It would do me no good to sting you because we both would drown if I did that." The frog agreed and was taking the scorpion across the pond when, in the middle of the journey, the scorpion stung the frog. As the two of them were sinking to certain death, the frog asked, "Why did you do that?" and the scorpion responded, "I'm a scorpion and it's just my nature."

Probably more books have been written on leadership than any other subject (I know that this isn't true, but it sounds good at this point). In 1959, Warren Bennis wrote that "Of all the hazy and confounding areas in social psychology, leadership theory undoubtedly contends for top nomination" (259). There are just as many definitions as there are theories about leadership so, just to make an executive decision, we are going to take a definition from Dickmann and Stanford-Blair to say that "leadership is a process of influencing others toward the accomplishment of a shared purpose or value" (124).

In their book, *Connecting Leadership to the Brain* (2002), Dickmann and Stanford-Blair further define leadership as having the following components: It is "a natural phenomenon that emerges from survival instinct, an elemental phenomenon that is continually forming and maturing in reaction to environmental contest, and nurtured phenomenon that is responsive to the human capacity for conscious reflection and decision making" (122). They view leadership as an open context—which is like saying it is a moving target.

However, they do list numerous components that are inherent in leadership (123):

1. Taking charge
2. Helping others achieve goals
3. Problem solving
4. Directing resources to a purpose
5. Showing the way
6. Facilitating the actions of a group
7. Exercising power and influence
8. Making things happen
9. Coordinating a collective effort

Leadership is interconnected to brain development, emotional intelligence, learning, communication, and similar concepts. (It must be noted that I am quoting Dickmann and Stanford-Blair, yet they did not quote me in their book. I am just hoping for a mention in their second edition.)

Let's take the nine components of Stanford-Blair and Dickmann (which sounds like a law firm) one at a time to demonstrate how humor can address each one, thereby helping develop leadership.

1. Taking Charge

During the Industrial Age, "taking charge" meant that an individual in a position of authority would tell subordinates what to do. Leadership has progressed to incorporate more participation, cooperation, and empowerment—hopefully. What this means is that leaders need to be willing to share power and this can be made easier by sharing experiences, information, and jokes. People (and students) do not like to be told what to do, so if leaders can integrate humor into the process, it makes everyone feel more comfortable and work more efficiently. The next time you are in a leadership position, try using a humorous icebreaker, like asking individuals to introduce themselves by saying the funniest thing they saw on TV or in the movies recently.

2. Helping Others Achieve Goals

Leaders and teachers obviously need to set goals to achieve results. This is not always a natural process for individuals, so some training may be necessary. Leaders can always go the route of strategic planning, but another way might be through the use of humorous videos. Avoid the typical training videos, at all costs. Be creative and find other sources. For example, commercials like the ones for IBM, Nike, and Dell show innovative ways to beat the odds in achieving goals. Another great video is something called *Microcosmos*. Don't laugh, but it is a movie about bugs and insects, up close and personal. Numerous sections in the video can be used as a metaphor for beating the odds or achieving goals. Here are a few examples: there is a thirty-second section on watching a dung beetle overcoming an obstacle, a long line of caterpillars following each other in perfect unison, and a colony of ants working feverishly to build an ant colony. Each of the video clips can easily be connected to emphasize your point through a little reflection.

3. Problem Solving

Puzzles are the ultimate problem-solving activity. Bring a puzzle to a meeting, class, or event. The more childish the puzzle, the better. In fact, anything having to do with Disney works well. Give everyone approximately five pieces and ask the group to "see the big picture" and tell you the subject of the puzzle. Almost always, the group will simply look at the five pieces in their possession to guess what the picture is, and only after some time will they cooperate with each other to put the puzzle together, thereby solving the problem. This activity should lead to several different reflective discussions. One of the best pieces of reflection was the quote by David Beckham who supposedly noted that he was proud after finishing a puzzle in a mere six weeks, because the box indicated two to five years.

4. Directing Resources to a Purpose

In order to direct resources to a specific purpose, a leader needs to be able to network. Establishing relationships with others is typically a key component for leaders and humor most certainly helps in this regard. One rule of thumb is to visit people in person whenever possible, instead of relying on electronic communication. Joking with others or sharing a laugh about work will help to build relationships and should help with resource allocation and direction.

5. Showing the Way

Showing the way can also be equated to visioning. Obviously, many books show how to complete a visioning process, but one process is to have individuals draw pictures of the future or their desired outcomes. Pictures do not have to be serious; in fact, the less serious, the better. Drawing can elicit some hidden talents, but more times than not, the pictures are humorous, while at the same time showing the group the way to go. For example, have individuals draw a picture of a vehicle that shows what the organization currently looks like and what it will look like in five years.

6. Facilitating the Actions of a Group

Have you ever sat in a meeting or been part of a group that liked to talk more than get things accomplished? (Of course you have, if you work in education.) Nothing brings a group closer together than sharing a good joke. As noted in subsequent chapters, research shows that humor is very successful at building community. One specific way to accomplish both goals of getting things accomplished and adding humor to the process is through a modified Delphi process. Have individuals respond to a question, problem, or situation by writing responses on butcher paper. Then, give colored dots to everyone. You can buy different kinds of dots, like ones with pictures on them, or use a computer to make your own. Each person gets three dots and can place them on any solution they want. You can put all three on one item or divide up your dots. This activity not only gets people up and walking around, but talking as well, many times about the silly dots. The Delphi process can take many different avenues at this point, but usually you use the top five items and repeat the process until you get down to one.

7. Exercising Power and Influence

Exercising power and influence may be an important component of leaders, but it is also a way to lose friends. Individuals like to be consulted or involved with making decisions. Allowing individuals to be part of a joke or allowing others to joke around themselves is the same as empowerment for decision making. Spend time at meetings, in class, or with your staff sharing the funniest movie you saw that week, or the best joke they heard. You can also ask individuals about any bad experience concerning the topic being discussed and you will get a number of humorous responses.

8. Making Things Happen

Leaders that are well liked can get more done—that is, they make things happen. According to the research, humor raises the popularity of leaders. Whenever I attend a meeting, class, or small gathering, I bring candy in a Harley-Davidson lunch box. The candy is awarded as prizes throughout the activity for good answers, for telling jokes, or just good behavior. The lunch box is also a great conversation piece.

9. Coordinating a Collective Effort

Humorous activities build community and collaboration, thereby assisting in a collective effort. Here are a few tips:

1. Always relate the jokes to the audience.
2. Do not let your message get lost in the jokes.
3. Tell the joke and move on quickly. Don't admire your work.
4. Tailor the jokes and activities to the size of the group, level of expertise, and culture. This means you need to do some homework and find these things out.

By using these activities associated with the leadership components, you build leadership capacity. Then, by establishing a rapport with your class or staff, you will be given more latitude to make mistakes; which is helpful to any leader. If you do make a mistake (and you will), joke about it. Here are a few lines that will work in most instances after your miscue.

- I am a professional, so don't try this at home.
- I meant to do that; it takes talent.
- It may take a few minutes to sink in, but that will be really funny tomorrow.
- We will look back on this moment someday and laugh but it will take many years.

4

Humor and the Brain or
Why Slurpees Give You Brain Freeze

For years doctors knew that laughter had healing effects on patients, but the exact cause was not always identified. However, Lee S. Berk, professor at the Schools of Medicine and Public Health, found in her research that laughter results in 1) enhanced respiration, 2) an increased number of immune cells, 3) an increase in immune-cell proliferation, 4) a decrease in cortisol, 5) an increase in endorphins, and 6) an increase in salivary immunoglobulin type A concentrations (Howard 2002, 170). Humor has a direct effect not only on the brain, but also many other parts of the body — that is, leading with mind, body, and soul.

MEDICAL RESEARCH AND HUMOR

Experts have been examining the relationship of humor and medical research for years. Michael Miller, director of the Center for Preventive Cardiology at the University of Maryland School of Medicine, reported that in a specially designed test, 150 heart patients were "substantially less likely to laugh in a variety of everyday situations than a group of 150 members of the control group who were free of known heart disease" (Fauber 2000, 2a). The correlational research is not based on a cause-and-effect finding, but people who laugh are less likely to have a heart disease. The conclusion is that laughing may be like exercise and a healthy diet in preventing heart problems. The theory is that laughing has some sort of benefit on the endothelium, the protective layer of cells that lines the inside of arteries. The bottom line is that laughing helps the endothelium, the cells then increase and provide better protection to the artery, arteries help the blood flow, and we are less likely to get heart disease. Makes you want to smile, doesn't it?

Robert Provine of the University of Maryland published a book entitled *Laughter: A Scientific Investigation* (2000). He used MRI brain scans to probe why people cannot tickle themselves to laugh. (I am sure that the government paid for the study.) Neuroscientists used the MRI to detect more neuronal activity in the somatosensory cortex, the part of the brain that registers touch, when you are tickled. Scientists found that laughter blocks the neural reflex that regulates muscle tone, hence the expression "going weak with laugher" (Begley 2000, 76). Scientists also found that tumors on the hypothalamus, which regulates our daily bodily functions like breathing, can cause uncontrollable laughter. Provine concludes that laughter raises the heart rate as much as aerobic exercise, lessens the perception of pain, and increases tolerance of discomfort. This means that if you found anything in this book to be humorous, then it is better than an aerobic workout and should be a tax-deductible medical expense. I don't want to make any false claims here, but I think that you might even be able to lose weight without working out—just read this book once a day. It would make a lovely birthday present to all of your friends—better than the Atkins diet and less controversial.

Many researchers have also concluded that laughter is also a social behavior, thereby connecting it directly to both the physical and psychological aspects of individuals. Consequently, people laugh more in groups than alone. Therefore, my suggestion is that you get hundreds of people together to read this book out loud. In addition, women laugh more than men, which may explain the following:

> A woman had to have a brain transplant and was asked if she wanted a man's brain or a woman's brain. She said she would rather have a man's brain because it had never been used.

HUMOR IS NOT A BRAINLESS ACTIVITY

Humor without content is not funny. It must be processed and put into context or it is simply another story. Context is typically handled by the right

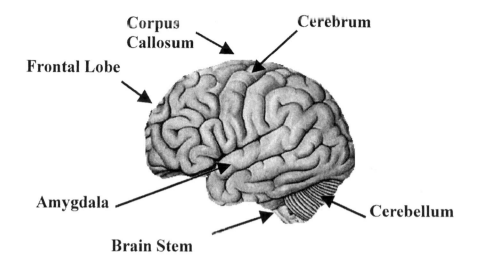

Lateral View

Figure 4.1.   Interior Parts of Brain

side of brain, while processing is completed in the left side of the brain. This is the same concept experts have discovered about learning from brain research: People must be able to apply learning by using the entire brain. The brain is divided into two hemispheres, the left and the right. A thick concentration of neural communication fibers known as the *corpus callosum* connects the two so that each hemisphere has its own processing styles and responsibilities yet communicates efficiently with the other. Using both sides of the brain facilitates cerebral activity, but most people do not use the entire brain as efficiently as necessary.

However, Sven Svebak (1977) writes that laughter helps both sides of the brain to function and produces a higher level of processing. He has even developed a "Sense of Humor Questionnaire," complete with reliability and validity. Similarly, William Fry (1986) writes that during laughter, people use both the right and left sides of their brains efficiently. Fry is a psychiatrist from California and has studied humor to find that twenty seconds of laughter is the aerobic equivalent of three minutes of hardy rowing (Culberson 2000). These researchers have come to the same conclusions as other researchers using an electroencephalogram, who found that when a joke is told the left hemisphere of the brain's cortex starts a sequence of chemical reactions that moves to the frontal lobe, or the center of emotionality. This is when the right hemisphere looks at the larger components of the joke, and it is all communicated through the corpus callosum to be captured by the occipital lobe. Catecholamine production is stimulated in the brain during laughter. Catecholamine helps improve alertness and memory. Consequently, humor improves the alertness of the brain and helps an individual think more creatively.

To demonstrate the activities and power of the human brain, try this activity. While sitting at your desk, make clockwise circles with your right foot. While doing this, draw the number 6 in the air with your right hand. What direction is your foot going now? This activity is a humorous demonstration that shows the connectedness of the brain.

Howard Gardner (1981) writes that human beings with damage to the right hemisphere of the brain do not laugh as much as healthy individuals. As noted, the right hemisphere synthesizes the information looking for connections, or analyzing the big picture. In 1999, Prathiba Shammi and Donald Stuss also researched the relationship of humor on brain damage. They found that the right frontal lobe most disrupted the ability to appreciate humor. Good to know, but how would you like to be a volunteer for this study? When people are laughing, the brain seems to operate more efficiently and symmetrically (Scriven and Hefferin 1998). "Humor seems to facilitate a more balanced cerebral activity that leads to creative thinking. This creative thinking produces different solutions to problems than the individual or group might otherwise generate" (14). Creativity is good, but not always. We do not want creative car driving.

Ultimately, the brain has three main functions: it is cognitive, reflective, and emotional. It is cognitive because people can learn—they can memorize facts and learn new material. The brain is reflective because individuals can analyze material. Information cannot only be learned but it can also be examined, put together with other information, dissected, and synthesized to make meaningful connections. And finally, the brain is emotional. In order for the brain to operate at its most efficient level, individuals need to have their emotions in check. For example, a person learns best when his or her emotions are elevated, but he or she is not too anxious or nervous. Humor helps provide the right level of emotional connection in establishing an atmosphere conducive to learning and leadership All three of the main functions of the brain need to be operating in unison.

As noted, individuals learn best when their emotions are on alert, but not in a state of panic. All sensory input for people goes first to the amygdala of the brain, which is the center of emotions. If the information proves not to be harmful to the person, it can then be processed in the normal fashion. Humor used at the proper time can assist in this process. For example, if individuals are bored or nonreactive, a good joke can be used to lift their emotions. In the same way, if groups are out of control, a humorous group activity should be used to bring down the emotional content. As a way of explanation, scientists conclude that when you laugh, your endorphin level rises in the body. This same response occurs as part of the survival instinct for anyone. Moreover, an increase in the endorphin level is also similar to an aerobic workout, so here we go again. Laughing is just as good as working out, and you don't have to shower afterward.

Humor is a universally accepted technique that elevates the emotions of an individual so the brain works more efficiently and will enhance the capacity for learning and leadership. Therefore, when you introduce humor into the environment, you can activate the brain, make it more aware, and put the amygdala on alert. Here are a few examples that may work well as overheads to be used when you need to adjust the emotional level of the group.

Question: What is the next line in this sequence?

1

11

21

1211

To figure out the answer, you should not be looking for mathematical equations, which everyone does. Instead, the answer can be found by saying the lines out loud. For example, the first line is read as "one, one," which is the second line. The second line reads as "two ones," which becomes the third line. The third line reads as "one two and one one," again which is the fourth line. The answer is 111221.

The next three lines would be:

312211
13112221
1113213211

Or you can try this one.

What order are these numbers in?
8
5
4
9
1
7
6
3
2

Most individuals will look for numerical patterns again, but you should instruct the audience to think outside the box by looking at the puzzle from all different angles. The answer is that the numbers are in alphabetical order, that is, eight, five, four, nine, one, seven, six, three, two.

Riddles are also good for activating the brain:

What is greater than God,
More evil than the devil,
The poor have it,
The rich need it,
And if you eat it, you will die

Answer: Nothing

Of course, in any activity, there are differences between the male and the female brains.

This overhead is great when discussing brain research, learning, differences between men and women, and similar areas of concern.

Now that you know how the brain works, you can use humor to help control the environment, thereby enhancing the learning and leadership.

THE FEMALE BRAIN

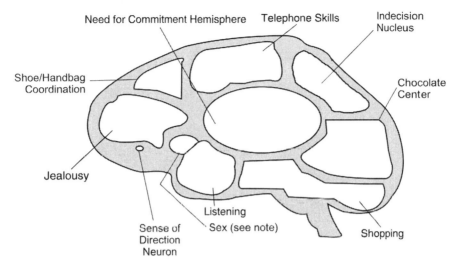

Need for Commitment Hemisphere   Telephone Skills   Indecision Nucleus

Shoe/Handbag Coordination

Chocolate Center

Jealousy

Listening
Sense of Direction Neuron   Sex (see note)
Shopping

Footnote: Note how closely connected the small sex cell is to the listening gland

Figure 4.2.   The Female Brain

THE MALE BRAIN

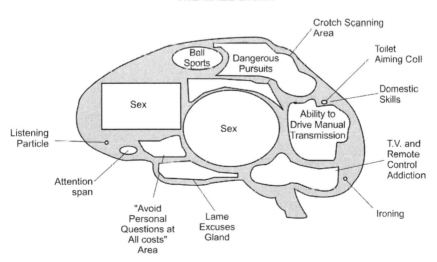

Crotch Scanning Area

Ball Sports   Dangerous Pursuits

Toilet Aiming Coll

Domestic Skills

Sex

Sex

Ability to Drive Manual Transmission

Listening Particle

T.V. and Remote Control Addiction

Attention span

"Avoid Personal Questions at All costs" Area   Lame Excuses Gland

Ironing

Footnote: the "Listening to children cry in the middle of the night" gland is not shown due to it's small and underdeveloped nature. Best viewed under a microscope.

Figure 4.3.   The Male Brain

Use the brains as overheads to interact with your colleagues, students, or staff when you need to raise the level of conscientiousness of the group. Carry the overheads around to important meetings and bring them out when you need to bring the group up or back under control with brain-friendly humor.

5

Humor and Learning or That's Not Funny, It's Teaching

David Sousa writes in *How the Brain Learns* (1995) that the brain is comprised of a trillion cells (give or take one or two). The nerve cells are called *neurons*, held together by the glial cells. Neurons are the main operating parts of the brain and the body's nervous system. A neuron has thousands of small "branches," called *dendrites* (from the Greek word for tree). There are a quadrillion connections (I believe that this might be an estimate) of dendrites in the brain. Just to give you an idea of this number, one quadrillion seconds is 32 million years. "The dendrites receive electrical impulses from other neurons and transmit them along a long fiber called the *axon*" (20). Neurons receive signals through a chemical reaction from other cells through the dendrites over a small gap, called a *synapse* (from the Greek term to join together) between the cells. Just like in the movie *My Big Fat Greek Wedding*, everything is derived from the Greeks. This electrochemical process can spread throughout the body in one-fifth of a second, while the neuron can transmit 250 to 2,500 impulses per second (20–21).

The brain can certainly learn new material, but it would rather connect it through previously learned information, because this makes the work of the neurons, dendrites, and synapse operate more efficiently. Nevertheless, it is interesting to note that people actually remember less than 1 percent of what they see, hear, feel, smell, and taste everyday. (This should help explain some of those low grades in high school.) Through the five senses of the body, the information goes to the area of the brain called the

sensory register, or the *reticular activation system (RAS)*, located in the
brain stem. Through a process of filtering, pertinent information for survival goes on to short-term memory and/or working memory. At any time,
if the brain decides that the information is useless (like reruns of *Survivor*), it is not stored or processed further. If the brain can make a connection to previous experiences or make sense out of the information and
if it fits into the cognitive belief system, then it may be stored in the long-
term memory—that is, we learn it. Survival and emotional data have pri-
ority over cognitive processing. The amygdala is always filtering information to see if it should raise an emotional response or if it is a danger
(again, reruns of *Survivor* fit this category). Sousa notes that the brain is
a "lean, mean, pattern-making machine." With more than 40,000 bits of
information going into the brain every second, it must decide quickly and
accurately what needs to be remembered, and why.

However, the brain does not really like details, and it would rather look
for trends or the "gist" of the material. This fits in nicely with the taxonomy of Benjamin Bloom, with knowledge (memorization of details) on
the lower end of the scale and evaluation on the higher end. For the brain
to make patterns, it needs to make connections with previous information
learned, and the material must be relevant. For the brain to be successful
at making patterns, the brain can typically handle about twenty-five minutes of a lecture. (How many teachers adhere to this brain-friendly way of
teaching?) We need to shift paradigms about learning because today education is very good at preparing students for the past. Moreover, the brain
likes protein, water, and sleep. After twenty-five minutes, your brain starts
thinking about the soccer game that your son is playing tonight or what is
on ESPN or if you left the coffee pot plugged in, not on the material being discussed.

PRACTICAL POINTS TO PONDER ON
MEETINGS, GROUPS, AND GATHERINGS

An important function of any leader is dealing with groups. Meetings,
classes, presentations, and gatherings should not only be well organized,
with an agenda, but any presentations should also be limited to twenty to
twenty-five minutes. Coffee and water should be made available, and

donuts should never see the light of day. Make the announcement of the meeting interesting by sending out ornate reminders with bells and whistles and clip art. Have humorous nametags for individuals or allow people to make up nicknames for themselves. I have even distributed cards with 1 through 10 written on them. As the meeting progresses, these select people can hold up the cards, like judges at a skating competition. They can hold up a 1 if things are going poorly, a 5 if it is just OK, or an 8, 9, or 10 if things are going great. This is not only good feedback for you but it introduces humor into the meeting.

Experts say that as a leader you have thirty seconds to set the tone of the meeting, class, or presentation. This is not a long time, so you must come out with passion and purpose. Do not start out with a general welcome or "Hello, it is so nice to be with you today." Your best bet is to quickly get to the point, explain the mission or purpose, or grab the audience's attention with a pertinent joke. The joke will set the tone of the meeting while addressing the topic. No matter what, be enthusiastic as a leader. Stanford University researchers found that a successful sale depends on 15 percent of knowledge and 85 percent on enthusiasm. Remember, the best meetings or speeches have a strong introduction, a dynamite conclusion, but more importantly the two need to be put very close together.

The brain likes connections and activities. Bring in props, visual aids, and gadgets to help. For example, if you are discussing a topic, bring in a model of that item—for example, the brain. The more outrageous looking the item, the better. I bring in wind-up toys to use throughout the meeting when input is low. I also have overheads of Dr. Seuss handy. Here is just one sample used when discussing technology or the Internet (50).

> So, as fast as I could,
> I went after my net.
> And I said, "With my net
> I can get them I bet.
> I bet, with my net,
> I can get those Things yet!"

In fact, ask participants to find their favorite Dr. Seuss quote for the next meeting. You will be surprised how innovative they can be.

ACTIVITIES

Allow the person taking minutes to integrate clever clip art or jokes. Nobody reads the minutes anyway, at least this way they can look for the jokes. Make people sit by height during the meeting or at tables with people who like soccer, baseball, reading, or whatever. Have people engage in activities during a meeting that are brain-friendly and serve a useful purpose. Play games like figuring out brainteasers from a puzzle book, or "wacky-wordy" puzzles. You can find examples on the Internet or in *Puzzle* magazine—for example, "now^{he}re" (which equates to, "he is in the middle of nowhere"). Games build cooperation and people have fun.

Another humorous and interesting activity is to write on butcher paper four or five items that may differentiate individuals—for example, the location of childhood: outside of the United States, city, suburbs, small town, or farm. Hang the signs up on the wall and ask individuals to move to the one that best describes them. Have individuals talk with the group about the topic of the meeting or problem being discussed. Then, take down the signs for place of birth and underneath should be a list of five different recreational activities: reading, sports, traveling, theater, or sleeping. Have individuals move again to the location that best describes them. Again, have people discuss the topic of the meeting or problem. This is one way to get the brain working more actively, demonstrate "diversity" among your staff, and get cross-culturalization of ideas.

You should bring candy or treats to a meeting. Give door prizes to individuals for small accomplishments. With a group that does not know me, I would ask for a volunteer and, as you know, many times people are afraid of volunteering. The old amygdala is working a mile a minute when this happens. Eventually you will get one brave soul to come forward and then simply give them a piece of candy, thank them for volunteering, and let them sit down. The moral of the story is that being first, or volunteering, may have its rewards, so do not think that it will always be negative. You will be surprised how fast you get a volunteer the next time. For more detailed examples, you might want to check out Sheila Feigelson's book, *Energize Your Meetings with Laugher* (1998).

One of the best ways to end a class or meeting is from Max Hitchins (as cited in Walters 1995). Hitchins often talks about how minds get locked and will not open up to new ideas. He asks individuals to sit upright in their chairs, with backs against the support, and feet squarely on the ground. Then, he asks them to try and stand up without leaning forward or moving your feet—it cannot be done. Max then asks individuals to bend their backs slightly forward. Everyone should be able to stand at this time because of the small adjustment. Everyone will be on their feet so you can then simply thank everyone for the standing ovation and conclude the meeting or gathering.

HUMOR AND MEMORY

The use of humor has a direct effect on memory and metamemory. The use of humor has been found to increase memory and metamemory judgments on delayed recall testing. In other words, individuals forget more and more details as time passes; however, humor can increase memory performance (Thompson 2001). You know the old saying that a picture is worth a thousand words? Well, individuals will remember humorous cartoons better than the literal translations of the information. There is even a connection between humor, increased memory, recall of sentences, and decreased heart rate. Humor helps individuals to remember information better and longer.

The majority of the research studies conclude that humor has a positive effect on the efficiency of memory. When someone laughs, he or she increases the intake of oxygen to the blood while exercising muscles, which ultimately produces endorphins in the body. Endorphins are described as nature's painkillers (Coleman 1992, 270). This type of physical response increases the efficiency of the brain and consequently can improve memory. Laughing helps memory, but there are other facts at work, like age.

It must be noted that memory is not always dependable. The brain can, and will, organize facts by creating many false memories by associating incorrect facts to situations. In fact, several studies concluded that an eyewitness may be one of the more unreliable forms of evidence available because of the unstable nature of memory—as much as 75 percent inaccuracy in details from eyewitnesses. Try showing a clip of a movie to your students and then give them a short quiz on the details to see just how accurate even short-term memory can be, or cannot be, trusted at times. Even if you warn students ahead of time, they will typically be very inaccurate in the descriptions. The bottom line is that learning and humor are complex entities that are both directly connected to the memory of individuals, but memory is not the only entity at work in either case (Zola 2003).

Humor not only enhances memory, it also can enhance problem-solving capabilities. For example, Glassman (1991), in his book *The Creativity Factor*, recounts the story of a mountainous region where winters are cold and rainy, where ice was forming on the power lines causing damage, and the local bears prevented the timely repair.

> A technician was complaining about being harassed by bears on a repair trip. One person jokingly suggested, "Let's train bears to climb telephone poles in winter to shake off the ice that breaks the transmission wires." A second person, again in jest, suggested, "Let's put honey on the tops of poles in winter so the bears will climb the poles and shake the ice off the wires." A third suggested, "Let's use helicopters to place the pots of honey on the poles to attract the bears." These comical responses led to the solution of using the downdraft from helicopters flying over the wires to knock the ice off the wires. (9)

The atmosphere of allowing humor to respond to work situations helped to foster creativity, thereby solving a work problem. Allowing humor to penetrate a classroom, meeting, or brainstorming session can allow more creative thinking in problem solving.

HUMOR AND LEARNING

Bob Marzano (2003), a national expert in research and learning, uses a methodology called meta-analysis in the book *What Works in Schools: Translating Research into Action*. A meta-analysis reviews the literature for quantitative research on a specific subject and then analyzes and synthesizes the results into comprehensive conclusions. Marzano concludes that other researchers have found nine main instructional strategies that affect student achievement: 1) identifying similarities and differences, 2) summarizing and note taking, 3) reinforcing effort and providing recognition, 4) homework and practice, 5) nonlinguistic representations, 6) cooperative learning, 7) setting objectives and providing feedback, 8) generating and testing hypothesis, and 9) using questions, cues, and advance organizers (80). By connecting humor to these nine areas, the learning process is enhanced. Part of the advantage of this scenario is that humor helps the individual associate the material to previous knowledge.

Now, how do you take what we know about humor and learning and put the two together? Two humor researchers, Scriven and Hefferin (1998), think they have the answers. They list six suggestions for using humor in the classroom:

1. Keep a book of jokes or cartoons handy and read something funny ten minutes before teaching a class.
2. Look for amusing anecdotes that can be used to illustrate difficult concepts.
3. Utilize analogies that transform abstract ideas into more familiar examples.
4. Use colorful expressions and homemade "props" to communicate important ideas.
5. Laugh at yourself.
6. Laugh with your students. Such laughter helps to promote a bond between a teacher and students. (15)

CONNECTING HUMOR TO LEARNING: THEORY AND PRACTICE

As you may notice, many of these suggestions by Scriven and Hefferin are directly connected to the research strategies suggested by Marzano about teaching in the classroom. Listed are the practical suggestions of Scriven and Hefferin on humor, matched to the theoretical structure identified by Marzano on learning, and accompanied with (hopefully) humorous examples.

1. Practical suggestion: Keep a book of jokes or cartoons handy and read something funny ten minutes before teaching a class.
   Theoretical Structure: Homework and practice
   Example: Practice makes perfect. Does anyone know someone who is perfect? No. Practice actually makes for improvement.

2. Practical suggestion: Look for amusing anecdotes that can be used to illustrate difficult concepts.

   Theoretical Structure: Reinforcing effect and providing recognition

   Example: While traveling through a small town in the South, a visitor saw an old man sitting on the porch of his house. He asked the man if he had lived here his whole life and the man replied, "Not yet."

3. Practical suggestion: Utilize analogies that transform abstract ideas into more familiar examples.

   Theoretical Structure: Identifying similarities and differences

   Example: The hammer Michelangelo used to create the Pietà was similar to the one used to destroy it. Or, there is more information in one edition of the *New York Times* than any one person would have received in an entire lifetime in seventeenth-century England.

4. Practical suggestion: Use colorful expressions and homemade "props" to communicate important ideas.

   Theoretical Structure: Nonlinguistic representations

   Example: Ask for a show of hands from the audience for those who want the lights turned up brighter. Then, turn the lights up in the room. Chinese proverb: It just goes to show that more hands make a task lighter. Or, as St. Francis stated, "Preach the gospel always and, if necessary, use words."

5. Practical suggestion: Laugh at yourself, which will help you to become one of the group.

   Theoretical Structure: Cooperative learning

   Example: Bearing a child takes nine months no matter how many people you assign to the task. Or, seldom does one piece of coal burn alone.

6. Practical suggestion: Laugh with your students. Such laughter helps to promote a bond between a teacher and students.

   Theoretical Structure: Laughing at yourself will help build relationships with students by reinforcing their effort and providing recognition. It also is a form of cooperative learning and even provides feedback.

   Example: Remember, honesty is the key to any relationship. If you can fake that, you are in (Courteney Cox on *Friends*).

Another strategy is to develop a list of jokes, stories, anecdotes, and so forth. With the advancement of technology today, it is relatively easy to input jokes you hear or read into a database organized by specific headings or categories. This will help you to connect the proper joke to the right story or content of a paper, speech, meeting, or learning environment. Writing down jokes or interesting stories will take some behavioral adjustments; however, it is not easy to talk yourself out of what you behave yourself into.

If you need further assistance, here are a few analogies that may help with the learning process from Frank Visco in *How to Write Good*.

My several years in the word game have learnt me several rules:

1. Always avoid alliteration.
2. Prepositions are not words to end sentences with.
3. Avoid clichés like the plague. (They're old hat.)
4. Employ the vernacular.
5. Eschew ampersands & abbreviations, etc.
6. Parenthetical remarks (however relevant) are unnecessary.
7. It is wrong to ever split an infinitive.
8. Contractions aren't necessary.
9. Foreign words and phrases are not apropos.
10. One should never generalize.
11. Eliminate quotations. As Ralph Waldo Emerson once said: "I hate quotations. Tell me what you know."
12. Comparisons are as bad as clichés.
13. Don't be redundant; don't use more words than necessary; it's highly superfluous.
14. Profanity sucks.
15. Be more or less specific.
16. Understatement is always best.
17. Exaggeration is a billion times worse than understatement.
18. One-word sentences? Eliminate.
19. Analogies in writing are like feathers on a snake.
20. The passive voice is to be avoided.
21. Go around the barn at high noon to avoid colloquialisms.
22. Even if a mixed metaphor sings, it should be derailed. (Visco n.d.)

In order to increase learning, information needs to be connected to previous knowledge or experiences (more brain stuff). In the educational system today, we have developed a labyrinth of standards, performance indicators, strategies, and rubrics. In leadership and humor, you must do the same. Reflect on the characteristics that you set as the standards of being a leader. Then, develop performance indicators on how you are going to reach the standards. Ultimately, you need a strategy for achieving the results and some sort of rubric for measurement of what is working and what is not; this leads to continuous improvement. Plan, do, check, act for the humor cycle, if you will—plan the joke, tell the joke, check for your reaction, and then act on the joke. There is a proverb from Ghana that states, "Tell the truth and run." But you cannot do this with humor. Look to see if you get the reaction you were hoping for and then readjust the joke or story for the next time. Reflection can go a long way, and this is one of the three basic functions of the brain.

One way to check your progress of humor is to simply provide a feedback form to your staff or students. Ask individuals to write down the three most important things learned and how humor helped. Another tool is the Real/Unreal Analysis. Have individuals take a piece of paper and draw a line down the center. On the left column, write down "real" possible solutions to a problem; in the right column, write down humorous, or "unreal" solutions to a problem. Or you can have individuals write down their feedback on the meeting or seminar in the left column, and in the right side column write down humorous comments about the meeting. The Real/Unreal Analysis works well for almost any activity.

Here is another brain-based activity that may be used to connect learning to humor. Have members of the audience or group list ten items from any topic or experience. Using the following list, take these items one at a time, put a number to them (one to ten) and in your head think of the most outrageous picture or story equated to the corresponding word. First memorize the following list.

One = bun
Two = shoe
Three = tree
Four = door
Five = hive
Six = stick
Seven = heaven

Eight = gate
Nine = line
Ten = hen

For example, if someone is listing items in a grocery store and the first one identified is a coconut then you think of the coconut as being number one. Remember, one = bun. Think of the coconut as being as big as a house and is inside of a bun for a giant to eat. You will remember coconut as being the first item (one = bun) through the image concocted in your head. You can do this for the entire list of ten items by being as outrageous as possible with the story or picture in your mind. Then, you can recite back the list in any order through association with the story or picture. This works for more than just ten items by using the same list but placing items eleven through twenty in New York and items twenty-one through thirty in Chicago, or whatever cities work for you.

TEACHING, LEARNING, AND HUMOR

Despite the differences in levels of education, another problem with learning and teaching is that the curriculum and teaching style have not changed much over the years (or centuries). If an engineer from the 1940s fell asleep like Rip Van Winkle and woke up in the twenty-first century, he or she would not be able to do the same job. However, if a teacher fell asleep in 1940, he or she could easily be hired in many school districts today. Just think how little different colleges today are from the Middle Ages. You know it took fifty years to get the overhead projector out of the bowling alley and into the classroom? Now, bowling alleys have more technology than classrooms. I am not saying that people in academe are slow to change, but schools still have essentially the same curriculum in colleges today as when Aristotle started the Lyceum in the fourth century B.C.E. (See, my History major did come in handy, Mom!)

Part of the problem is not only the teaching style and pedagogy being used but the curriculum. In addition to not being brain-friendly, some faculty do not take the time to update curricula; it is not always on the cutting edge, but more like the bleeding edge. Sometimes it is easier to move a cemetery than it is to have faculty change curriculum.

Take, for example, the curriculum at the famous state school for animals. The administrators developed the curriculum, which was based on the state standards of running, swimming, and climbing. (This is another true story.) Three students enrolled in the first class: a bird, a squirrel, and a duck. The duck could swim very well, but he could not run or climb. He spent all his time on the latter two courses and could no longer swim. Eventually, he flunked out. The bird could obviously fly very well, but she flew to the top of the tree, instead of climbing. She set a record, but did not follow instructions and was kicked out of school for insubordination. The squirrel could swim well enough not to drown, run a little bit at a time before tiring, and he could climb just fine. He received two Ds and an A but he ended up being the valedictorian. Mediocrity wins out.

Moreover, even with updated material, many faculty still lecture like they did in the Middle Ages (and some faculty are as old as the Middle Ages), despite the fact that people remember about 10 percent of what they hear, 30 percent of what they see, 70 percent of what they do, and 90 percent of what they teach. Unfortunately, too many teachers rely on lecturing and using the strategies of "sit and get," "drill and kill," or "sage on the stage" instead of being the "guide by the side."

HUMOR AND LECTURES

Studies have found that college students who were presented with one of four lectures, using varying degrees of humor, and tested immediately after the lecture did not indicate an improvement in retention of the material. However, groups tested six weeks later showed an increase in retention of information for the students who had the lecture with humor related to the concepts (Kaplan and Pascoe 1977). Moreover, Desberg (1981) found that college students rated humorous lectures as being more enjoyable than humorless lectures in an educational setting. Consequently, the use of humor did improve appeal and teaching effectiveness.

However, the devil is in the detail, especially in education. Humor has been found to be highly correlated with insight, while humorous examples and illustrations in college texts appear to have no effect on information and motivation, a positive effect on appeal, and a negative effect on ability to persuade. Interestingly, sexual humor by male instructors was positively associated with teacher evaluations, but it had a negative effect for female instructors. Others have found that faculty use humor 3.5 times in a typical college class—but remember, humor must be relevant to be successful. In fact, nonrelevant humor can hinder the retention of information.

Many researchers have also found that humor is related to motivation, information processing, and enhancing learning. Laughter suppresses posterior hypothalamic activity, thereby allowing the cerebral cortex to reduce stress prior to completing an activity. Ultimately, with humor, "teaching and learning are more enjoyable, satisfying, and interesting" (Littleton 1998, 42). For example, individuals who laugh prior to completing a problem-solving activity are more successful than individuals who do not laugh prior to the test.

Marshall Tribble (2001) wrote that by using the AIME (Amount of Invested Mental Effort) students rated humorous presentations as less believable than nonhumorous presentations and rated themselves as more efficacious when learning from humorous instructional videos than with learning from nonhumorous instructional videos.

> A man dies and goes to the pearly gates where he meets St. Peter, who asks the man if he wants to go to heaven or hell. The man replies that he wants a preview. In heaven he sees quiet bliss. In hell he sees wine, women, and song. He selects hell. Once there, the devil hands him a shovel to stoke the fire and the man says "What about the wine, women, and song?" The devil replied, "Oh, you must have seen the video."

The study also found that humor is generally perceived as an easier, better way to learn, while also requiring more effort in order to comprehend content. Tribble obviously learned an important lesson: that you can make more of an impression if you come up with an acronym for your work, for example, AIME. Therefore, we are now going to label my findings in this book as HILARIOUS: Humor, Intellectual Learning And Research Innovations Offering Unique Strategies.

In research there are three rules that may apply to the above findings. The rules are listed here, along with the translation from a "non-researcher's" perspective.

1. "By analyzing all of the research, a definite trend is evident . . ." (These data are practically meaningless.)

2. "The mixed conclusions resulted in great theoretical and practical importance . . ." (It may only be of interest to me.)
3. "While it has not been possible to provide definite answers to these questions . . ." (The results really are mixed, but I still have to get it published.)

PRACTICAL POINTS TO PONDER

Listed are the five main components of how humor can be used to enhance learning, along with practical, and less-than-practical, examples.

1. Empowering learners: Use laughter to bring students into the learning and teaching process.
   Example: Have students bring in jokes to start the class or have staff bring in jokes to a meeting. Before you start class or a meeting, have one person read a joke. Humor can break cultural and gender barriers. It tends to make the world smaller and more intimate.
   Nonpractical example: A kindergarten teacher was observing her classroom of children while they drew. She would occasionally walk around to see each child's work. As she got to one young girl named Katie who was working diligently, she asked what the drawing was. Katie replied, "I'm drawing God." The teacher paused and said, "But no one knows what God looks like." Without missing a beat, or looking up from her drawing, the girl replied, "They will in a minute."
2. Thinking creatively: Use humor to be more creative and more innovative.
   Example: Bring in prompts that are innovative to help students and staff. Use a picture of a camera to tell people to "stay focused" or an orange juice to "concentrate."
   Nonpractical example: We always want people to think creatively, but putting a statue of a cow next to a blue spruce is not creative landscaping, except in certain states that will remain nameless (Tennessee).
3. Generating interest: Students appreciate humor and consequently take a greater interest in class.
   Example: Have individuals complete a questionnaire on their activities, favorite comedy show, funniest story about themselves, funni-

est relative, and so on. During meetings or a class, allow individuals to read one of the stories to lighten the mood. This activity also helps you as a leader or teacher to get to know your students and staff.

Nonpractical example: Mel was talking to her teacher about whales. The teacher said it was physically impossible for a whale to swallow a human because even though it was a very large mammal its throat was very small. Mel stated that Jonah was swallowed by a whale. Irritated, the teacher reiterated that a whale could not swallow a human; it was physically impossible. Mel said, "When I get to heaven I will ask Jonah." The teacher asked, "What if Jonah went to hell?" Mel replied, "Then you ask him."

4. Enhancing self-esteem: Humor can help students to be part of the group and enhance their self-esteem.

   Example: Do not try to please everyone in the group. Alfie Kohn writes that you cannot really motivate others because internal motivation is more powerful than extrinsic motivation. As a leader, you should simply provide the atmosphere conducive to learning, and humor will help by providing a positive culture.

   Nonpractical example: It is frustrating when you know all the answers, but nobody bothers to ask you the questions. Remember, laugh at yourself and you will always be amused.

5. Emphasizing socialization: Once again, humor helps students become part of the group, open lines of communication, and make friends. Laugh with someone and it builds relationships, but tell a joke to make someone laugh at you, then it is a power relationship (Pollak and Freda 1997).

   Example: Ask people to tell the most interesting story about themselves as an icebreaker. You go first so the group feels comfortable. Without even emphasizing humor, you will get several funny stories.

   Nonpractical example: In Wisconsin you wear hunting clothes out to formal occasions and for true socialization.

6

Four Theories of Humor or
It Makes Sense in Practice but
Does It Make Sense in Theory?

Humor has been a popular topic of research for many years. The first researchers concentrated on observations concerning the effects of humor. In the 1970s, researchers expanded their vision to examine the psychoanalytical foundations of humor based on the works of Freud. Interestingly, Freud wrote in *Jokes and Their Relation to the Unconscious* (1905/1960) that he was a proponent of how humor can reduce tension and anxiety by theorizing that humor allows for socially acceptable expressions of aggressive impulses (Brooks 1992, 7–9). Today there are many ideas about why humor works, but four main theories have emerged: incongruity theory, relief theory, superiority theory, and cognitive theory. The incongruity theory emphasizes practical and intellectual foundations, while the relief theory relies on the affective nature of the joke, the superiority theory has many psychological ramifications, and the cognitive theory relates back to knowledge, learning, and the brain.

WHY HUMOR WORKS

Theory #1—Incongruity Theory

"If you can't convince them, confuse them!" (Harry S. Truman)

Incongruity theories are basically cognitive in nature and explain humor as unexpected or surprising experiences, words, or activities that happen.

Strange, absurd, inappropriate consequences or endings are examples of incongruity theories.

> A basketball player was having difficulty getting into college. The academic dean said that if the coach would fill the arena with alumni and the student passed a test in front of this crowd, under all that pressure, he would be accepted to the college. One week later, 50,000 alumni crammed into the arena and the student met the academic dean at mid court. The dean said, "I am going to ask you one question and if you get it correct, you will be accepted into the college. The question is what is four times four?" The student said, "Sixteen," and 50,000 people moaned at the same time, "Oooooohhhhhhh, nooooo. Give him one more chance."

Practical Point to Ponder

Throughout the day there are going to be times when teachers and leaders are confused, your students are confused, or your staff is confused. Do not hide it, joke about it. Too many times leaders try to cover up the unknown by pretending to know the answer or just ignoring the problem. The best way to solve a problem, resolve a conflict, or ease the confusion is to hit the situation head on, and joking about the problem puts people at ease.

Theory #2—Relief Theory

"Most of us are willing to change, not because we see the light, but because we feel the heat."

The relief theory has physiological foundations dealing with the affective aspects of humor and is also known as the psychological theory. The reduction of tension and anxiety are main components of the relief theory and can be tied directly to basic functioning of the brain (Brooks 1992, 10). The brain is a wonderful thing; it starts working when you are born and never stops until you get up to speak in public. In the same vein, according to *Newsweek*, people are more afraid of public speaking than dying. Jerry Seinfeld jokes that people are so afraid of speaking in public that at a funeral they would rather be in the box than delivering the eulogy. So, it is a relief that you are reading this book and are not dead or speaking in public right now. The relief theory is also known as a *coping mechanism*.

Practical Point to Ponder

When you are in a tense situation, the amygdala in your brain is working overtime and this could have negative physical, emotional, and intellectual effect. Sometimes, humor can, and should, be used to help. Memorize a few jokes to lighten the mood, and it also helps put you back into control while helping to calm any fears. The amygdala likes a good joke every now and then.

Theory #3—Superiority Theory

"It is frustrating when you know all the answers but nobody bothers to ask you the questions."

The superiority theory may be the oldest humor theory in history, with roots back to the ancient Greeks. Humor can be viewed as a weapon or tool of people to feel better than others, to attack or make fun of others, to feel superior, or to triumph over another individual (Brooks 1992, 9). The superiority theory may be demonstrated by Keith Harrell, a motivational speaker. He tells the story that in 1992, the marketing department of a large company called a meeting of its 10,000 staff. The marketing director took the stage and with tears in his eyes and said, "I just got the word that corporate is laying off 40,000 people. In three months, 80 percent of you will not be here." One person raised his hand and said, "I have a question. After these 80 percent are gone, can I have a bigger office?"

> One day George Bush, Bill Clinton, and Ross Perot found themselves at the gates of heaven. When they talk with God, he is sitting on his throne. God said to George Bush, "Who are you?" He responds, "I am George Bush, the ex-president of the United States." God responded, "You may sit on my right-hand side." He then asked Clinton, "Who are you?" and Clinton responded, "I am Bill Clinton, also a former president of the United States." God said, "You may sit on my left-hand side." God then asked Ross Perot, "Who are you?" He responded, "I am Ross Perot and you are sitting in my chair."

As noted previously, timing is everything and the joke was much funnier in the twentieth century when Perot was more of a political figure, but the names can always be interchanged with current figures.

Practical Point to Ponder

Many individuals use humor as the sword that cuts. Using sarcasm to cut down others, to make fun of people, or to ridicule may get a laugh but it is almost always destructive when building relations and in a leadership position. The only time that cutting humor works is when you have a very close relationship with the target of your joke and the audience knows about the close relationship; otherwise, stay away from criticizing others with humor.

Theory #4—Cognitive Theory

"I describe the present and because so many people have not arrived here, to them it sounds like the future."

The cognitive theory deals with everything not covered in the other three theories, but more importantly, the humor revolves around intellectual jokes, stories, puns, and so forth. Some humor is funny because of the cognitive or intellectual content and context. Cognitive humor works because people like to think; they like the intellectual challenge of figuring out puzzles, mazes, and complex jokes. In addition, individuals like to use their humor, and sometimes show off their intellectual abilities, through the use of jokes.

> A young bully decided to show up a smaller boy one day by playing a trick on him. The boy put a nickel and a dime in the palm of his hand and offered it to the smaller boy. When the smaller boy took the nickel, the bully laughed at how stupid the kid was. In fact, the bully told all of his friends about this trick and how the smaller boy, time and time again, took the nickel over the dime because it was larger. A friend asked the boy why he kept taking the nickel. The smaller boy said that he knew the dime was worth more, but if he had taken the dime the bully would have stopped trying to trick him. As it was, the smaller boy had made $2.00 off of the bully.

Practical Point to Ponder

As noted previously, humor has to connect with the audience. If the jokes are too highbrow (sometimes, like Dennis Miller on *Monday Night Football*) or if they are too sophomoric (like most of the attempts of humor in this book), the audience will get frustrated. Here are two ways to stay in touch with the audience. First, do your homework. Get to know your staff or students. Listen to what they are saying and talking about. Remember, from listening comes wisdom and from speaking comes repentance. Or you can give them a little quiz to find their likes, dislikes, what they do in their spare time, and so on. Then take notes on the reactions of your audience, class, or staff. Do not be afraid to even ask people if something is funny. I go around testing out stories, jokes, activities on my family and friends. If it is funny to a select few of your friends, it should work with your class or colleagues.

All four of these theories on humor have their roots in history. In fact, a multiplicity of historical lessons are found in this book. Remember, learning new things today does not make what we did yesterday wrong, it makes tomorrow better. For example, did you know that houses in the 1500s had thatched roofs with thick straw? Up on the roof was the only place for small animals to get warm. When it rained, many of the animals would slip off the roof, hence the expression "it is raining cats and dogs." The floors of the house were typically made of dirt, which brought into being the expression of being "dirt poor." However, many of the richer families had slate floors and would put straw or thresh down to help guests from slipping. Sometimes, the straw would be dragged outside and many homeowners would put a piece of wood by the door to stop straw, thereby becoming known as the "threshold."

Of course, all of these items are trivia. The term *trivia* comes from the Middle Ages where three (tri or trivium) roads would come together. It was at this point that most traffic would pass. Therefore, people usually posted notes, messages, or posters. Hence, the name *trivia*. Leaders should use humor, respect history, and understand that trivia can be an interesting form of communication.

People like trivia. It makes you look more intelligent. When applicable, the use of trivia can be funny and help develop rapport with a group of people. Memorize a few pieces of trivia and slide them in when you can. It shows that you are well read (or have at least read this book), that you are knowledgeable, and trivia breaks down barriers for networking. People appreciate learning something they can use immediately. You can always help in the learning process by saying something like: "Go ahead and use that tidbit, free of charge."

Practical Point to Ponder

Write down a few pieces of trivia, puns, or pithy sayings on note cards. Use a hole-punch in the corner and tie them all together. In this way, you can carry them around to be used when necessary. Of course, an easier way is to put the same information in a PDA file.

MYTHS OF USING HUMOR

Although there may be four main theories about why things are humorous, there are also several myths about humor, according to the research. You should know these myths to help with integrating humor into leadership and learning.

Myth #1: If Something Is Funny Once, It Will Always Be Funny

Remember: If the horse is dead, dismount. Do not force a joke. If something stops being funny, stop using it. This means that you must pay close attention to the audience to see its reaction. This is nothing different than a leader or teacher paying close attention to their staff and students to provide the appropriate leadership or teaching styles. Also, remember not to step on your own joke. If you use humor, wait for the laughter to die down before you jump back into the message. Less is better sometimes.

Myth #2: Always Start a Meeting or Speech with a Joke

You do not always have to start out with a joke; in fact, it is more important that the humor be connected with the content of the material and have relevance to the people. It does not matter where you use humor, it is more important that it be used appropriately, matching the variables and theories listed.

Myth #3: Something Funny in One Setting Will Be Funny in Another Setting

Know your audience, but also know your setting. A state educational conference is different during a budget crisis than when everything is going well. Moreover, the time of day is also crucial to using humor. Adults can handle humor in the morning, but individuals under eighteen typically do not. Adults can handle humor at almost any time, but the evening is better than the morning. And finally, if you waste time telling long jokes, adults will resent it more than kids.

Myth #4: You Have to Make Everyone in the Room Laugh

A major problem for some people is that they tell a joke and one person in the room does not laugh. You then spend the next hour watching that person, trying to get him or her to laugh. Whether working with one person or a large group, do not think that you can get everyone to laugh every time. In fact, some people may not be the kind who laugh out loud at all. I used to have one staff member who never, ever laughed at anything that I did, but more than once he told me how funny I was. You just never know.

Myth #5: "I Can't Be Funny"

Wrong! Everyone can learn to be funnier. You may not wind up on *Saturday Night Live*, but you can learn the tricks of the trade to integrate humor into your daily activities, speeches, meetings, or conversations. You didn't know how to drive when you were fifteen, but you learned. Like leadership, there are certain characteristics and concepts to learn and you can make it happen.

Myth #6: You Have to Be Funny the First Time You Use Humor

Were you a great teacher the first time you taught a class? Were you a great leader the first time you took over a group? I don't think so. Take it slow, one day at a time, or one joke at a time. In fact, if you make a mistake, or something is not funny, do not leave it hanging out there. Admit it, "Geez, I am going to have to talk to my writers about that joke." Or if no one laughs, say something like "I wasn't really trying to be funny, I was going for the sympathy vote here. How did I do?"

Myth #7: Every Joke Has to Be Funny

Wrong again. Do not push too hard with a joke. Even if you think that it is the funniest thing in the world, if people do not laugh, give up on it. Do not keep telling the joke just because you think that it is funny. People will let you know if it is humorous or not.

Myth #8: You Have to Be Careful Not to Offend Anyone with Humor

Wrong! You can, and you will, offend someone. It is like being a leader—sooner or later, you are going to make someone upset by your decisions or actions. Deal with it. You cannot be tentative when using humor. You should obviously try to avoid offending someone, but if you are tentative or not sincere, people will know it. You might want to record yourself when using humor. Listen to the words on the tape, the timing, and more importantly, the reaction of the audience. Again, people will let you know if something is funny.

Myth #9: Humor Has to Deal with Fictitious Items

The truth is not necessarily humorous but it can be. Humor does not have to deal with the extraordinary and grandiose. If this were true, half of the comedians would be out of business. Here is a quick tip about being funny: just tell the truth and simply exaggerate the details. Or you can simply take the alternative view of a situation to be funny. You can talk about driving to work in the morning and how you almost hit a bird, but explain it as driving with one eye on a bird that was twice the size of a 747 when all of a sudden it dived-bombed your car probably because you had a sticker advocating education for everyone. The bird must have been a Republican.

Myth #10: Humor Will Work in Any Situation

Unfortunately, this is not true. When you are dealing with a very delicate situation, like a hearing for any type of serious misconduct, humor should not be used. As a leader, you need to use discretion—but there are times it is better to err on the side of not using humor than trying it and making the matter worse by being accused of not taking the situation seriously. (Many of these ideas come from *Learn How the Pros Make 'em Laugh*, 2001.)

Leadership and Humor or
Once You Get People Laughing,
They'll Listen to Anything

Once you get people laughing, they're listening and you can tell them almost anything.

—Herbert Gardner

Many authorities have written that books on leadership are simultaneously inadequate as well as grandiose in their conclusions. No author or expert has been able to come up with a definitive definition of leadership or demystify the concept in general.

As noted previously, "leadership is a process of influencing others toward the accomplishment of a shared purpose of value." Howard Gardner (1995), an expert in learning and leadership, writes in *Leading Minds: An Anatomy of Leadership* that four main factors are essential for effective leadership; they include: 1) a tie to a community or audience, 2) a rhythm in life that includes isolation and immersion, 3) a relationship between the stories leaders tell and the traits they embody, and 4) the centrality of choice. These four factors encompass many of the leadership characteristics outlined by many other experts. Moreover, they serve as a defining point for establishing the parameters of leadership, and how humor can be connected.

TIED TO A COMMUNITY OR AUDIENCE

Leaders need to not only be part of a community, they need to be fully connected to the community and cannot exist without followers. The relationship between leader and follower must be active, ongoing, and dynamic (Gardner 1995). The same rationale that makes this an accurate statement is true for being able to connect humor to leadership aspirations. Humor has to be connected to the community. Several years ago, I was consulting with McKay Nursery in Waterloo, Wisconsin (I am plugging the company because I need several new bushes for the side of my house). Being from the "big city" of Milwaukee, I wanted to relate to the audience comprised of small-town, hard-working outdoorsmen, so I told the following story to break the ice.

> Two good friends went to Alaska hunting bear. They were flown into a deserted part of the state. After one week, the pilot returned and each hunter had bagged a bear. The pilot said, "I cannot carry you and the two bears in the helicopter, it is too heavy. Someone should have told you that one is the limit. The mountains are too high to fly over with this load." One of the hunters pleaded with the pilot, indicating that last year the pilot was able to load both bears and two hunters, so apparently this pilot was "chicken." Not backing down from a challenge, the pilot loaded both bears and they took off. After only six miles, the helicopter crashed. No one was hurt but one hunter looked at his friend and said, "That wasn't too bad because we made it farther than last year before crashing."

This story demonstrated an understanding of the culture and climate of the nursery, and I thought I might be accepted as a member of the group and as an outside consultant. Of course, you do realize that you are never an expert in your own backyard. I call this the "sixty-mile principle," where you must travel at least sixty miles away from home to be considered an expert in any area. McKay Nursery is sixty-one miles away from Milwaukee, so I was safe.

RHYTHM OF LIFE

Gardner writes, "A leader must be in regular and constant contact with her community" and must be able to "find the time and the means for reflecting, for assuming distance from the battle or the mission" (36). Gardner defines a "rhythm of life" as a leader knowing where she is going and what she is doing. The leader is dedicated and immersed in a vision or goal and has a balance in life. This same concept is true with humor, where you must be in regular and constant contact with your community and know where you are going with the jokes. There must be a rhythm in leadership and with humor.

Leaders are able to make lemonade out of lemons (I just *had* to get this phrase in somewhere). How do you hold a hundred tons of water in the air with no visible means of support? You build a cloud. A rhythm in life means that leaders must use their vision to find answers and unique solutions to problems. They are confident of where they are going and work until they find the right answers. Leaders rise to the occasion and then promptly sit down.

One of the best examples of living a balanced life, or leading with rhythm, comes from my pet dog. Here are the things we can learn from a dog about leadership:

- Never pass up the opportunity to go for a joyride.
- Allow the experience of fresh air and the wind in your face to be pure ecstasy.
- When loved ones come home, always run to greet them.
- When it's in your best interest, always practice obedience.
- Let others know when they've invaded your territory.
- Take naps and always stretch before rising.
- Run, romp, and play daily.
- Eat with gusto and enthusiasm.
- Be loyal.
- Never pretend to be something you are not.
- If what you want lies buried, dig until you find it.
- When someone is having a bad day, be silent, sit close by, and nuzzle him or her gently.
- Delight in the simple joy of a long walk.
- Thrive on attention and let people touch you.
- Avoid biting when a simple growl will do.
- On hot days, drink lots of water and lie under a shady tree.
- When you are happy, dance around and wag your entire body.
- No matter how often you are criticized, do not buy into the guilt thing and pout. Run right back and make friends.

RELATIONSHIP BETWEEN THE STORIES LEADERS TELL
AND THE TRAITS THEY EMBODY

A key component of connecting humor to leadership is that there obviously has to be a relationship between the story and point that you are making. "Leaders exercise their influence in two principal, though contrasting, ways: through the stories or messages that they communicate, and through the traits that they embody" (Gardner 1995, 37). The lesson here for humor is to make a connection and to use humor that is true to your own nature. This will help establish your leadership style. One of the best ways to make a connection between humor, leadership, and salient points is through the use of stories.

Doug Stevenson is a story-theater professional and a national consultant in the area of humor and storytelling. Stevenson's work (2002) is an example of teaching with humor, while integrating brain-friendly techniques. He lists the following five areas that make storytelling important to learning.

1. Connect people with a common experience—people need the left brain and right brain to communicate.
2. You get inside the story and feel it; otherwise, people get screensaver eyes.
3. Set up the story, but then get in and out quickly.
4. Fit the story to the audience.
5. Use the writing formula, not writing. Write like you speak.

Stevenson has been able to connect humor, storytelling, and learning all in one by using many of the concepts of brain research to tie them all together in a meaningful manner. Although the brain is designed to make connections, all of its operations and purposes should be viewed in total, not as separate working functions. The brain is one complete organ with separate entities working in unison. Learning is enhanced in the brain through connections to relevant material. While analyzing a story, the brain works as one entity to construct data, create meaning, create new experiences, and learn. Although there are many ways to assist in the learning process, storytelling has been identified as one of the best methods to enhance learning through brain-friendly methods. Stevenson merely uses everyday, common stories, adds humor, and connects the message to previous learning to make a point, thereby making the process an excellent tool for leaders.

Listed are his steps in the story structure process:

1. Set the scene in step one: Create the context for the story. Set time, location, weather and conditions. What was going on emotionally, physically or spiritually?

2. Introduce the characters: Help me to see them with visual descriptions. Tell me about your relationship, their quirks. Become them. Do this with key characters only, not everyone. (See character development below)

3. Begin the journey: What is the task, the goal, the journey? Where do you have to go? Who do you have to connect with? What is the challenge?

4. Encounter the obstacle: Without conflict, the story will be boring. The obstacle may be a person, a challenge to overcome or a self-limiting belief. Exaggeration here will make it funny.

5. Overcome the obstacle: What did you have to do to overcome? What strength did you have to summon? Perhaps your helper is the hero, perhaps it is you. Be specific. Break your solution down into a few steps in sequence. This is where the teaching happens.

6. Resolve the story: Tie up any loose ends and make sure your audience knows how everything turned out. Go back over your story for logic and hear it as the audience will hear it.

7. Make the point: It is important that your story has one clear point. Too many points confuse the issue. One story, one point. Make it simple and easy to remember. This is where you work in your "Phrase That Pays."

8. Ask the question: Make your story their story by asking the question. "Has that ever happened to you?" Turn the point into a question. Push their buttons. The question makes your story pertinent and adds power to your point. (Stevenson 2002)

Here is a key to connecting humor to leadership. Research points to communication as a major component, and by using storytelling you are able to appropriately use humor to fit the situation. People can learn to communicate more effectively, learn to be leaders, and certainly learn humor.

For example, my wife and I have three kids, and you know how it is with kids. With the first one, we bought one of those toys where you put round pegs in round holes. As soon as Katie put the first one in correctly, we got out the video camera and called the television station with excitement. When our second child, Mel, figured out that the round peg goes into the round hole as I was walking by her one day, I said, "Hey Nancy, look what Mel did." When our third child was in middle school, I said to Nancy one day, "Hey, did we ever buy Kevin one of those toys with the round pegs and round holes?" The moral of the story is that integrating humor into leadership takes commitment.

It should come as no surprise that the most meaningful stories come from reality. One of the best stories depicting the consequences involved with humor, leadership, and change, transpired in November 1964. In Sweden at 4:15 p.m., everyone had to pull over on the side of the road and stop driving their cars for a half hour. They then changed the side of the road they were driving on. It just goes to show that "sometimes you have to pull over and pause before you change directions," which may be necessary in learning how to use humorous stories.

THE CENTRALITY OF CHOICE

Leadership is derived through the choice of people, not through force or by the position that a person attains. Management, on the other hand, is a much more position-oriented concept. Moreover, in order to be a leader you need to have followers. Humor is the same—neither leadership nor humor can be forced; no matter what you think, the recipients will decide if you are a leader and if you are funny.

The stories of Tom Shackleton and Edward Scott are examples of both management and leadership. Interestingly, Scott accomplished his goal and Shackleton did not, yet the latter was much more of a leader because of his actions, not his position. Scott is one of the first people to reach the South Pole, but in true English style he did it by the book, adhering to the rules no matter what. He refused to deviate from standard operating procedures, even when they made no sense. For example, he swabbed the deck at the same time everyday, even if it was freezing outside. He may have made it to the South Pole but he lost many men in the process. Shackleton, on the other hand, is known for *not* making it to the South Pole, but he was able to be a true leader, even as his boat was crushed by the ice. Eventually, he led some of his men 900 miles in a small boat in the high seas to a cold whaling station on a deserted island to get help. He went back to get the rest of his men and lost none to the cold and terrible weather conditions in the process. Shackleton was a true hero and leader. To be successful, Shackleton was innovative and was a leader by his actions. Too many times we do not think out of the box, we simply make the box bigger.

Research confirms that change happens from the bottom up as people closest to the situation are able to make decisions and unite for a common cause. Harley-Davidson Motor Company is a prime example of centrality of choice and leadership empowerment. Jeff Bluestein, former CEO of Harley-Davidson, explains that everyone within the company is treated as a leader. After all, don't the employees successfully lead their own lives? Why not allow them the same respect and responsibility at work? Bluestein says that in order to build a true learning organization, a leader should be a coach, a trainer, and a facilitator, not a dictator. This type of thinking has earned the company national respect and recognition. Bluestein was the choice of the people partially because he interjects humor into his leadership style, which makes him more accessible and one of the group. He was respected even more when he purchased his Harley-Davidson from a dealership and had to wait like every other customer.

Becoming the leader of choice cannot be rushed or forced, and humor is one way to assist in the process. However, trickery is also good, and as the author of this book, I have no problem resorting to this level. Here is a way to get a group to feel they are in sync (not like the boy band). Have everyone work separately and quietly on this task. Have them pick a number between 1 and 10. Then, multiply the number by 9. Be sure to give the non-math people time to complete the task. Add the digits together, for example if you have 27, it would be $2 + 7 = 9$. Subtract 5 from whatever number you have. Now, carefully associate your number with a letter of alphabet—for example, 1 = a, 2 = b, 3 = c, and so on. Here is the tricky part, think of a country that starts with the letter that you have chosen. Remember the name of the county. Take the last letter of the country and think of an animal that starts with this letter. Remember both the country and animal. Take the last letter of the animal you have and think of a color that starts with that letter. Now be sure to tell the group that "if you are a good crowd and are all thinking alike you will have an orange kangaroo from Denmark." This will work about 90 percent of the time and is a great way to grab the attention of your audience while demonstrating your leadership abilities.

PRACTICAL POINTS TO PONDER

As noted previously, the key is to use the anecdotes or stories to enhance learning. The following are suggestions on how to use humor and integrate it into leadership of schools:

1. Humor can be used to establish boundaries of groups (Barecca 1991; Crawford 1994).Warren Bennis noted that Howard Gardner believes "The right anecdote can be worth a thousand theories" but it uses up a thousand times more memory. Styles of humor and practical jokes that are not acceptable within a group let you know a great deal about the culture and intellectual boundaries.
2. Humor can be used as a motivation tool and helps build teamwork. Good-natured joking about a mistake puts individuals at ease, and leaders who use humor when they make a mistake help to motivate others to try something new or to take chances. Remember, an ounce of pretension is worth a pound of manure.
3. "Phony or polite laughter as a response to humor should also be a signal to a leader or teacher that an uncomfortable situation exists or that communication is not succeeding" (Coleman 1992, as cited in Wallinger, 1997, 31). Learn to read your staff or students. They will not only give verbal and nonverbal feedback on your leadership, or teaching methods, they will certainly give you feedback on whether humor is working or not.
4. "Humor reinforces the absurdity of rigid, inflexible behavior and misunderstanding and helps us remember that mistakes are natural and widespread in all humanity" (Weinstein 1986; Berger 1993; Crawford 1994, as cited in Wallinger, 1997, 31). The days of dictatorial leadership are gone. Humor breaks down the old industrial barriers of top-down leadership.
5. "Cognitive skills and background experiences increase as we become adults, thus providing fertile ground for viewing situations and prob-

lems in a humorous light" (Crawford 1994, as cited in Wallinger, 1997, 33). The same jokes or humorous activities that work for elementary students do not work for adults. You need to have an "arsenal" of jokes, puns, overheads, activities, and similar tactics.

6. Humor can make life more productive and tolerable. Use jokes when things are going well and also when they are not going so well in the leadership role. Just like in sports, never get too high with the victories or too low with the defeats.

7. Humorous stories or examples help people remember important information. Do not overdo the use of poignant stories. If everything is made to be a joke or very important, then nothing will really be important.

8. People are eager to learn the outcomes of stories so they will pay attention. Real-life stories actually work better than fictitious stories. Make them short and sweet with one main point. Most people carry PDAs. Use it to take notes on funny events and activities throughout the day so that they can be integrated into your leadership activities at the right time.

9. Humor can unite members of a group and help persevere in even mundane tasks (Wallinger 1997). Have a humor board at work or in the classroom. Allow individuals to bring in funny stories from the newspapers to post them on the board. You would be surprised to see the number of unusual or humorous situations people get into.

10. Use historical and clever sayings to make a point. For example, here are a few that almost everyone should be able to relate to. Use them in an unusual manner, to start a story, or to emphasize a point.

    a. For score and seven years ago . . .
    b. I'll be back (in the voice or Arnold Schwarzenegger)
    c. I shall return . . .
    d. Here's looking at you, kid!
    e. Interchange words to help sell your point, "Ask not what you can do for humor, ask what humor can do for you."

8

Leadership Tools or If You Only Have a Hammer, Then Everything Is a Nail

If there is a lesson to be learned in this book, it is that humor is tied directly to learning and can be used as a leadership tool. After reviewing and synthesizing all of the research on humor, there are six main ways to use humor to improve or enhance leadership skills, knowledge, and action.

1. Humor and communication
2. Humor and emotional intelligence
3. Humor and the organizational environment
4. Humor and teamwork, socialization, and/or relationships
5. Humor and change
6. Humor and stress or anxiety

The remainder of this chapter deals with the first topic, humor and communication, while subsequent chapters cover the additional aspects of humor.

HUMOR AND COMMUNICATION

There is little or no doubt (unless you read this book) that humor enhances communication, communication enhances leadership, and therefore humor enhances leadership. (This is true, if I have my logic correct from freshman-year philosophy class.) Leaders use humor to communicate to colleagues, staff, and organizations by reinforcing positive behavior and discouraging negative behavior. Communication is probably the most important tool that can be used by leaders.

Let's get specific. Listed here are six suggestions on how to use humor to increase communication (Gruner 1985). Remember, "Humor competence can be considered the fifth component of the theoretical framework for communicative competence" (Vega 1990, 1).

Suggestion #1

The humor used appropriately will help produce a more favorable reaction for the leader (adapted from Gruner 1985, 142).

Duuuuhhhh. This one is not really an earth-shattering conclusion; however, as normal human beings, we need—and want—the approval of others. While part of the relationship factor deals with trust, part of it entails the development of strong communications. Allow me to elaborate.

> One day I convinced Don W. (a colleague) to work with me as a consultant on strategic planning for a small school district in northern Wisconsin. Don was not happy to give up a Saturday driving up north but he did it as a favor to me. And as is my habit, I was running late, making Don wait in the car for about thirty minutes before we could start on the long drive. We were behind schedule and things only got worse. I was driving fast in order to make up for lost time, but being the king of coffee I told Don that I had to stop to get some "liquid fuel." Late and mad, Don only reluctantly agreed. As we were leaving the parking lot, I noticed that a police car turned its red lights on behind me. I was speeding only a little but did not have my seat belt on. As I pulled over to the side of the road, I did what every red-blooded American would do, I surreptitiously strapped the seat belt on, hopefully without moving my head or shoulders to let the officer see what I was doing. When the police officer approached, I asked, "What's wrong?" He said it is the law in Wisconsin to have your seat belt on. I said, "Well it is on now, so I was sure it has always been on, and besides, I have a witness." Don was sitting in the front seat with his arms crossed looking down at the ground, fuming. The officer leaned over and asked, "Sir, is this correct? Did the driver have his seat belt on?" After a long pause, Don slowly lifted his head and grudgingly said, "If Peter said he had his seat belt on, he must have had his seat belt on. I have learned not to argue with him after he has been drinking." It is all about relationships and communication.

Suggestion #2

Self-disparaging humor will enhance the leader's image, while self-promoting humor has the opposite effect (adapted from Gruner 1985, 142).

I would provide an example here but, being a perfect speaker and writer, I have no examples. For this particular suggestion, Gruner cites a Chang and Gruner (1981) study (don't you love it when an author cites his own research?) in an experiment using a psychologist and an economist. (You know that if you lay all of the economists down in a straight line, they still would all be pointing in different directions.) I would give you the details of the research but suffice it to say that ($p <$ .10) on authoritativeness, and significantly higher on "domineering" than data on the economist, except on Tuesdays when ($p < .05$) and when the B (beta) had a linear regression of R^2 greater than 17. In other words, college students love it when the teachers are willing to make fun of themselves. Self-deprecating humor is much more acceptable to students than humorous comments from leaders who are egotistical or self-promoting—like the one who opened this suggestion. People appreciate humorous leaders, but not leaders full of hubris, no matter how funny they may be.

Suggestion #3

Apt and relevant humor can increase the interest and novelty of a leader (adapted from Gruner 1985, 143).

Humor increases the level of interest in communication, thereby enhancing the level of acceptance of the individual. However, there is a "ceiling effect," where you can have too much of any good thing. In economics they refer to this as the law of diminishing returns. Moreover, humor may help with communication, but the message needs to be appropriate, have the right content and, of course, the interest rating of the material must have a direct correlation on the use of humor. Go for the joke and keep making connections, but if you find yourself with material that does not work, stop using it. It is like the old saying where the definition of stupidity is doing the same actions over and over again, but expecting different results. Used wisely, humor can make you and your message more interesting; after all, most students think that teachers cannot be funny, so just by attempting humor you will be appreciated.

Suggestion #4

Appropriate humor can have a positive influence on the effectiveness of persuasive communication by leaders (adapted from Gruner 1985, 144).

You have to understand that there are at least two different generations in schools today. Teachers are usually from the baby boomer era, while students in the schools are more of the generations X and Y eras. Having been brought up on computers, fast food, MTV, and digital everything, students of today really do not need to be entertained in school, but they do want innovation, technology, and action—not the same old lecture format. Humor provides that change of pace and novelty.

Figure 8.1 is an overhead that I use on many occasions when dealing with students of any age, or anyone who has ever been a kid. Some people give the credit of the development of these rules to Charlie Sykes, a conservative radio talk-show host in Milwaukee, while others give credit to Bill Gates in a speech to Whitney High School in Visalia, California. I am going with Bill Gates because he has more money. The author explains eleven things that students will not learn in school. He writes about how feel-good, politically

Figure 8.1.   Rules of Life

Rule 1: Life is not fair—get used to it.

Rule 2: The world won't care about your self-esteem. The world will expect you to accomplish something *before* you feel good about yourself.

Rule 3: You will *not* make $40,000 a year right out of high school. You won't be a vice-president with a car phone until you earn both.

Rule 4: If you think your teacher is tough, wait till you get a boss.

Rule 5: Flipping burgers is not beneath your dignity. Your grandparents had a different word for burger flipping—they called it opportunity.

Rule 6: If you mess up, it's not your parents' fault, so don't whine about your mistakes, learn from them.

Rule 7: Before you were born, your parents weren't as boring as they are now. They got that way from paying your bills, cleaning your clothes, and listening to you talk about how cool you are. Before you save the rainforest from the parasites of your parents' generation, try delousing the closet in your own room.

Rule 8: Your school might have done away with winners and losers, but life has not. In some schools, they have abolished failing grades and they'll give you as many times as you want to get the right answer. This doesn't bear the slightest resemblance to *anything* in real life.

Rule 9: Life is not divided into semesters. You don't get summers off and very few employers are interested in helping you find yourself. Do that on your own time.

Rule 10: Television is *not* real life. In real life, people actually have to leave the coffee shop and go to jobs.

Rule 11: Be nice to nerds. Chances are you'll end up working for one.

correct teachings create a generation of kids with no concept of reality and how that concept will set them up for failure in the real world.

The list contains elements of humor, along with a real message that may be more easily remembered. As a matter of fact, lists are a great way to integrate humor and leadership. Look at the success David Letterman has with his top-ten lists. See appendix C for numerous examples of humorous lists to use.

Suggestion #5

Humor will make a speech or message more "memorable" and the message more long-lasting (adapted from Gruner 1985, 144).

There have been numerous research studies on this particular topic with varying results, which makes it tough to come to any kind of conclusion. Therefore, I will do what any good researcher would do: ignore the data that contradicts my conclusions. Humor not only helps the audience enjoy a class, speech, or meeting more, it helps them remember the message with advanced immediate recall, as well as better recall of the content in the long run (Kaplan and Pascoe 1977). In one quasi-experiment completed at the end of a statistics course, faculty who used humor had students scoring 15 percent higher on an objective test than students in a nonhumorous condition (Ziv 1988b). These results are very interesting, but it must be questioned what a statistics teacher thinks is humorous. Moreover, you must also realize that a quasi-experiment is one that is not really an experiment. It is like saying $2 + 2 = 5$ for extremely large values of 2. Actually, there is a great book entitled *Statistics for People Who Think They Hate Statistics* that integrates humor into a statistics textbook, so it can be done.

Suggestion #6

When using humorous satire in a form of communication, be sure to know the level of intelligence of your audience (adapted from Gruner 1985, 144).

Researchers have found that intelligence seems to be related to the ability to understand satire. I am not quite sure that I understand this point, but it must be interesting (*psych!*). Research on the use of satire has actually found inconsistent results, which is really a researcher's way of saying "I just don't know what the answer is but really wish it would support my ideas."

Vinton (1989) not only agrees with the research of Gruner by support-ing the concept that humor enhances the levels of communication, but he also developed a taxonomy. (Of course, you know that once you develop a taxonomy you increase the sales of your book, even though no one re-ally knows what a taxonomy is. I think that it has something to do with the practice of stuffing and mounting wild animals.) Vinton's research found that humor can best be divided into the following levels: 1) puns, 2) goofing off (slapstick), 3) jokes/anecdotes, 4) humorous self-ridicule, 5) bawdy jokes (sexual or racial bias), and 6) teasing/bantering. I am one of five kids in my family and can tell you that every one of the six levels of "humor" was employed in my house almost every day of the year, typ-ically against me. My parents were great but they got tired of yelling and enforcing all of the rules by the time my youngest brother was in his teens. In fact, the only rule left in the house for my youngest brother was that there were to be no semiautomatic weapons in the living room.

By using any of the six levels of humor, Vinton claims that humor ful-fills the need for socialization into the group by improving communica-tion. This may be true but you need to use humor in an appropriate fash-ion. Using humor inappropriately can be damaging. Bob Dole knew his own level of humor and had the right idea with the title of his book, *Great Presidential Wit Laughing (Almost) All the Way to the White House.* To-day, the quantity of information doubles every eighteen to twenty-two months; by 2005, it is estimated that information will double every three months. Therefore, it may be increasingly more difficult to discover the intelligence of the audience, so you need to keep researching and reading about what makes people tick. The best advice here is to constantly read periodicals that depict the culture, music, humor, and entertainment of the "younger" generation.

Remember that the real art of communication is not only saying the right thing in the right place but also leaving unsaid the wrong thing at the tempting moment. One excellent resource to help with saying the right thing at the right time is Lilly Walters's book, *What to Say When . . . You're Dying on the Platform: A Complete Resource for Speakers, Trainers, and Executives* (1995). Walters provides numerous jokes, antidotes, stories, and so on, but more important, she provides instances in which they should not be used.

9

Humor and Emotional Intelligence or
If It Looks Funny and Feels Funny,
Then It Is Funny

Emotional intelligence involves the ability to perceive accurately, appraise, and express emotion; the ability to access and/or generate feelings when they facilitate thought; the ability to understand emotion and emotional knowledge; and the ability to regulate emotions to promote emotional and intellectual growth.

—Salovey and Sluyter 1997, 10

Some facts about humor and emotional intelligence: The more you understand and can control your own emotions, the more you can relax. The higher your level of emotional intelligence, the more you will take chances and laugh at more diverse types of humor. As children grow and mature, their sense of humor also develops. Moreover, as people increase their level of factual knowledge, their development of symbolic, logical, and abstract reasoning skills, as well as their humor production, also increases (Masten 1983). However, the older you get does not necessarily mean that the smarter and more humorous you get—but there is a theoretical connection between your emotional intelligence and your age, gender, intelligence, and sense of humor.

Moreover, most people believe that there is a difference between men and women when it comes to emotional intelligence and humor. This is an important point to know as you use humor with various groups in teaching. To help in this regard, here are a few definitions by gender.

commitment (ko-mit-ment) n.

    female: A desire to get married and raise a family.

    male: Not trying to pick up other women while out with one's girl-friend.

communication (ko-myoo-ni-kay-shon) n.

    female: The open sharing of thoughts and feelings with one's partner.

    male: Scratching out a note before suddenly taking off for a weekend with the boys.

entertainment (en-ter-tayn-ment) n.

    female: A good movie, concert, play, or book.

    male: Anything that can be done while eating.

remote control (ri-moht kon-trohl) n.

    female: A device for changing from one TV channel to another.

    male: A device for scanning through all seventy-five channels every 2.5 minutes.

vulnerable (vul-ne-ra-bel) adj.

    female: Fully opening up one's self emotionally to another.

    male: Playing football without a helmet.

Many researchers have found that leaders (superintendents or principals) fail not because of their lack of knowledge in specific areas in curriculum development, budgeting, or technology, but because of a lack of interpersonal skills accentuated by little or no emotional intelligence—a failure to get the best out of people who possess necessary information (Kets de Vries 1990). Don't forget that "failing" really means "Finding An Important Lesson Inviting Necessary Growth." Leaders should not fear failing and should learn to keep their emotions in check. After all, "fear" is really "False Evidence Appears Real." The following story further defines fear and emotional intelligence.

> There once were two Buddhist monks walking on a long journey. You must remember that Buddhist monks are not only celibate but they may not even touch a woman. As these two men approached a wide river, they met a woman who could not cross the water. Without speaking, one of the monks picked up the stranger and carried her across on his back. Nothing was said by the other monk until at the end of the day when they were setting up camp for the night. The one monk said, "How could you have carried that

women, as it's forbidden?" The other monk said, "My friend, I put her down hours ago, you are still carrying her."

Jean Piaget, a leading educational authority, believes that there is a relationship between cognitive development in change and humor comprehension (Mooney, 2000). Piaget and other developmental psychologists believe that emotional and intellectual development can depend on being confronted by discrepancies in family backgrounds. In other words, the more you learn, the more you understand humor. So, hopefully you are laughing more as you read this book because then it shows how smart you are becoming, thereby supporting the theory. Humor has the ability to be distinguished from general intelligence and verbal ability (Feingold and Mazzella 1991). Moreover, intelligence, creativity, and humor are all correlated and can develop together over time (Hauck and Thomas 1972). Consequently, the smarter you are, the more creative you tend to be, and the more humorous you can be.

Humor can both enhance and hinder the learning process, depending on whether the humor is used with the right connections—that is, affecting the emotional intelligence. Edwards and Gibbony (1992) cite fifteen principles discovered in their research for using humor in the college classroom. The bottom line is that people must use emotional intelligence with humor to be most effective (Edwards and Gibbony do not use the words *emotional intelligence*, but I want to have a smooth transition to the next paragraph).

FIFTEEN PRINCIPLES FOR USING HUMOR IN THE CLASSROOM

1. Teachers can encourage laughing at humorous circumstances to build a feeling of unity.
2. Teachers can use humorous examples and present concepts to help students comprehend and retain material.
3. Humor should be appropriate to the situation and contain the personality of the leader. You must be yourself. Students and peers will see through fake enthusiasm.
4. Teachers might not want to use humor in anxiety-producing situations.
5. The target of humor should be something or someone other than students. Detachment from the humor is always good.

6. Teachers should take special care to avoid self-disparaging humor. (While Edwards and Gibbony list this item as one of the fifteen principles, I disagree. If you are a competent instructor or leader, and gain the respect of students by your teaching skills and knowledge, self-disparaging humor can work very well. It makes the instructor more personable.)

7. Even though humor that has female targets is perceived as funnier than humor that has male targets, caution should be used so as not to perpetuate sexist notions. (This is actually true of any subject. In today's politically correct mania, every topic must be considered carefully before being part of humor.)

8. Male instructors can use almost all types of humor to increase their evaluation ratings.

9. Female instructors should avoid the use of puns or they are likely to greatly decrease their effectiveness ratings.

10. Female instructors might be able to increase their appeal ratings but not their overall evaluations by using hostile, especially sexually hostile, humor. This is one of the few positive correlations between female instructors and use of humor. (The research indicates this conclusion, but take this one with a grain of salt.)

11. Teachers who establish high immediacy through behaviors other than humor might not want to use a high degree of storytelling because it could be seen as a digression.

12. Teachers can use funny stories related to the topic to improve students overall attitudes. (The same results have been found with the use of technology.)

13. Male instructors can use topic-related humor to increase their ratings, but female instructors who use topic-related humor will achieve only marginally higher ratings.

14. Male instructors can use humor that distracts students from the class topic and still achieve high evaluations, but female instructors who do so will likely be rated lower in appeal, effectiveness, and delivery.

15. To be perceived as effective by students, instructors should use humor that adds to the content of education and contributes to the point (Edwards and Gibbony 1992, 22–23).

Individuals using humor must address the emotional intelligence (and age) of the audience. And in the same vein, individuals must not take situations too seriously and need to use a sense of maturity when interpreting humor. Maturity and age are intertwined.

Here are stages of maturity for individuals, associated with the stages of humor:

At age 4 maturity is . . . not wetting in your pants.
At age 4 everything is funny.

At age 12 maturity is . . . having friends.
At age 12 everything is funny, except if it relates to you.

At age 16 maturity is . . . having a driver's license.
At age 16 everything is funny, except things relating to you and your parents, who are just sad.

At age 20 maturity is . . . having sex.
At age 20 humor comes second only to sex.

At age 35 maturity is . . . having money.
At age 35 only Democrats are funny.

At age 50 maturity is . . . having money.
At age 50 Republicans are now looking funny.

At age 60 maturity is . . . having sex.
At age 60 nothing is funny, except Social Security.

At age 70 maturity is . . . having a drivers license.
At age 70 everything is funny, except jokes about old age, sex, religion, and politics.

At age 75 maturity is . . . having friends.
At age 75 everything is funny, especially old age, sex, religion and politics.

At age 80 maturity is . . . not wetting in your pants.
At age 80 everything is funny, but you are not sure why.

Emotional intelligence is sort of a barometer for gauging what humor works with a select group or individual. The higher the emotional intelligence quotient for someone, typically the more accepting they are of humor, and the more they will laugh at themselves, and with you.

10

Humor and the Organizational Environment: A Management Tool or He Ain't Funny, He's My Boss

Over the years, numerous authors have examined organizational structures and cultures. Experts like Thomas Sergiovanni, Margaret Wheatley, Tom Peters, Peter Senge, and others have probed, prodded, explored, and explained almost every component of an organization from it being a learning environment to operating in "chaos." However, few of these experts have examined the relationship of organizations to humor. Nevertheless, the effect of humor on organizations can be dramatic by reducing tension, entertaining, building rapport, sharing positive feelings, and controlling behavior (Gunning 2001). Ultimately, effective leaders need to match the right tool to the right situation because if all you have is a hammer, then everything looks like a nail. Humor in the right situation can influence the workgroup in a positive manner (Duncan, Smeltzer, and Leap 1990).

Learning organizations need to have balance or equilibrium, which is related to the second law of thermodynamics. My son, Kevin, learned the second law in sixth grade, but few adults seem to remember it. Kevin calls thermodynamics the "laziness law"—the tendency of closed systems to wear down, to give off energy that can never be retrieved. This is the main concept within strategic planning, where organizations need to keep changing and improving and not rely on the status quo to get better. If an organization is not a lean, mean, changing machine, then it will not survive. Continuous improvement is not just an expression but a way of life. Ecologist Garrett Hardin aptly paraphrases this concept as the following: "We're sure to lose. Life goes on, but it's all downhill." Humor can keep it all fresh and maybe prevent the organization from going downhill.

Strategic planning is one of those buzzwords where everybody thinks that their organization is required to do, but they are not sure what it is. Few organizations are actually successful at strategic planning. New consultants come in to your organization, change a few terms around (is it strategies, objectives, or goals?), they add a new twist, and sell it as the latest, greatest form of planning. My friend Don calls it the BOHICA syndrome: Bend Over, Here It Comes Again. For leaders, strategic planning is like going to a wedding, everyone gets excited about the event, and they have a great time at the reception. However, the hard work begins after the honeymoon, and that is where it all falls apart. Fifty percent of all marriages end in divorce, but I bet that 95 percent of all strategic planning ends in divorce. Today, because so many efforts have failed, employees see strategic planning like a funeral: Everyone gets all dressed up to go through the ritual, but they would rather not be there, and once it is over, they try to forget about it. Like strategic planning, humor has to be the accepted norm and practiced on a daily basis and not be just a separate entity. Half-hearted efforts like the ones used in strategic planning will not work with humor.

HUMOR AND ORGANIZATIONAL CULTURE

Humor "helps people appreciate their own culture, laugh about it a bit and share it with others, stereotypes and all" (Simons 1997, 2). Simons lists several guidelines to use humor in a multicultural world that will enhance the organizational climate.

1. First-person experiences are usually the best because they help relate a human side of the story and will be less offensive to others.
2. People should use humor to lighten up a delicate or controversial situation, not make fun of it. No one likes to be the aim of someone else's humor; sorry, Don Rickles. People can bond by sharing humor.
3. Ask others for their perspective of the situation or any humorous story, and they immediately become part of the group. For example, when you have a new class, ask them to say something about their

strengths and goals or aspirations and then ask them for an interesting, unique, or humorous story about themselves. As the teacher, you should go first and then the activity makes the students more comfortable and hopefully more emotionally stable in a sometimes stressful environment.

4. Study humor. Numerous Internet sites provide jokes of the day or interesting stories that can be used to help build culture. Just like teaching, using humor takes preparation—and just like teaching, the same lesson plans do not work year after year, nor do the same tired jokes. Why did the chicken cross the road? Because he was too lazy to find a new ending to the story. You get my point.

Humor is not only part of the organizational culture, it is an integral component. On a Monday morning after a great weekend, do you ask your friends about world news or do you relate interesting and humorous stories from the weekend? The soccer stories of your kids are only interesting to you, but a good joke will run through an organization in a matter of hours. How fast does a great joke travel over the Internet today? You probably get the same joke from two or three people in a matter of days. Humor can bring people together and help them to survive or succeed in their environment. More importantly, humor is a way of developing culture, keeping outsiders at bay, and defining norms within a group. As soon as a newcomer to your school or organization starts telling jokes, your group of friends includes him or her; they become part of the group and privy to the "inside" jokes. As a leader, you need to take this concept to the entire organization as one way to build culture.

I happen to live in Wisconsin, and jokes relating to the Green Bay Packers are a uniting force of the culture anywhere in the state. In fact, they are a part of the religion in the "frozen tundra." However, as good football fans, we do not tell derogatory jokes about the Packers, only the opponents. This would be sacrilegious:

A devout Packer fan died and went directly to heaven (that's where all Packer fans go, you know). He asked an angel if there were any former Packers in heaven. The angel replied, "Sure, all the greats are here." He then asked the angel if they played football and the angel replied that in heaven, every day is Packer Sunday and the Pack always wins. Just then the fan saw a man with dark-rimmed glasses, a heavy overcoat, and a cap that looked strangely like the one Vince Lombardi wore in the Ice Bowl. When asked excitedly if that was the coach, the angel replied, "No, that was God. He just thinks he's Lombardi."

Here is another example:

John Elway, after living a full life, died. When he got to heaven, God was showing him around. They came to a modest little house with a faded Broncos flag in the window. "This house is yours for eternity, John," said God. "This is very special; not everyone gets a house up here." John felt honored. On his way up the porch, he noticed another house just around the corner. It was a three-story mansion with a green and gold sidewalk, fifty-foot tall flagpole with an enormous Packers logo flag, and in every window a sign that read, "Cheeseheads." John looked at God and said, "God, I'm not trying to be ungrateful, but I have a question. I was an all-pro quarterback, I won two Super Bowls, and I even went to the Hall of Fame." God said "So what do you want to know, John?" "Well, why does Brett Favre get a better house than me?" God chuckled, and said, "John, that's not Brett Favre's house; it's mine."

Humor can also be negative by preserving differences between people, or enforcing a culture of repression. We all know that some kids make fun of other kids on the playground. We have all seen way too much violence in the schools over the years because of treating a child as an outcast and harassing those who are not part of the "norm." Adults can be just a cruel at times with the use of ridicule or satire. Humor can certainly build community, but it can also be a double-edged sword. Humor can even be used to hinder cultural cohesiveness.

A Packers fan in a bar leans over to the guy next to him and says, "Wanna hear a joke about Minnesota Vikings fans?" The guy next to him replies, "Well, before you tell that joke you should know something. I'm 6 feet tall and 220 pounds and I'm a Vikings fan. The guy sitting next to me is 6' 2" tall, 240 pounds, and he's a Vikings fan, and the guy sitting next to him is 6' 5", 280 pounds, and he's a Vikings fan, too. Now, do you still wanna tell that joke?" The Packers fan says, "Nah, not if I'm gonna have to explain it three times."

Learning organizations create an environment in which it is safe to take risks, employees feel they are empowered, and individuals are encouraged to try new things while not being criticized for making mistakes. After all, Thomas Edison failed more than 10,000 times to invent the light bulb, so it is a good thing that he never gave up or was yelled at for "screwing up" (pun intended). Being successful at using humor takes work and dedication, just like being a successful leader or inventor. Let's stay with Thomas Edison for the next example:

> Edison came into his office one day after running experiments for many weeks straight. He looked exhausted and his wife finally convinced him to take a vacation. Edison said, "But I don't know where to go." His wife replied, "Think of any place in the world where you would really love to be, and go there." The next day he went back into his office with his experiments.

CREATING BONDS THROUGH HUMOR

It is a natural instinct of people to belong to groups. People are social creatures and humor helps in this process. Abraham Maslow is obviously the most noted individual supporting this concept with his hierarchy of needs: physiological needs, safety needs, belonging needs, esteem needs, and self-actualization. Your need to belong to a group can be addressed by telling jokes and being told jokes. Therefore, if humor can help in this regard, the employees are more content and comfortable and then consequently might work harder and help the bottom line of the company—that is, profits or education.

In addition, humor appears to create bonds among the employees and to facilitate the accomplishments of work tasks (Vinton 1989). One time I was working with a local manufacturing company to help them to develop a strategic plan. (Somewhat ironic given the previous story.) The company employed only about fifty individuals, so it made communication relatively easy, and the organization was willing to change rapidly. The CEO, Roger, was a hands-on kind of leader who empowered employees. One day I asked Roger what he considered to be the main goal for the company for next year. Roger responded, "To make more money." I then asked for their goals for the next five years, and the response was "To make gobs of money." I chuckled at this, but when I randomly selected employees and asked the same question, I received the same response time and time again; humorous and very telling about the culture of the company. Money may be the root of all evil, but it sure can be a motivator and avenue for humor. However, the cost of living hasn't affected its popularity. It is like the bumper sticker that reads "I owe, I owe, so off to work I go."

Individuals use laughter to escape and handle problems calmly and effectively. One study found that 84 percent of the respondents to a national study of personnel directors at 100 of the nation's largest corporations believe that "people with a sense of humor are more creative, less rigid, and more willing to try new ideas" (Scriven and Hefferin 1998, 14). Take the example of a college professor:

A philosophy professor started class by picking up a very large and empty mayonnaise jar, filling it with rocks about two inches in diameter. He then asked the students if the jar was full. They agreed that it was. The professor then picked up a box of pebbles and poured them into the jar. He shook the jar lightly. The pebbles, of course, rolled into the open areas between the rocks. He then asked the students again if the jar was full. They agreed it was. The professor picked up a box of sand and poured it into the jar. Of course, the sand filled up everything else. He then asked once more if the jar was full. The students responded with a unanimous "yes." The professor then produced two cans of beer from under the table and proceeded to pour their entire contents into the jar, effectively filling the empty space between the sand. The students laughed. "Now," said the professor, as the laughter subsided, "I want you to recognize that this jar represents your life. The rocks are the important things your family, your partner, your health, your children—things that if everything else was lost, your life would still be full. The pebbles are the other things that matter like your job, your house, your car. The sand is everything else. The small stuff. If you put the sand into the jar first," he continued, "there is no room for the pebbles or the rocks. The same goes for your life. If you spend all your time and energy on the small stuff, you will never have room for the things that are important to you. Pay attention to the things that are crucial to your happiness. Play with your children. There will always be time to go to work, clean the house, and fix the disposal. Take care of the rocks first—the rest is just sand." One of the students raised her hand and inquired what the beer represented. The professor smiled. "I'm glad you asked. It just goes to show you that no matter how full your life may seem, there's always room for a couple of beers."

In another survey of 600 top executives from a variety of corporations in 1997, 100 percent of the executives stated that humor was important and healthy in a business situation, 99 percent of the executives would like their leaders to develop a greater sense of humor, 88 percent of the executives indicated that a lack of humor can be a sign that the company has morale problem, and 43 percent believed that the use of humor is decreasing (Scriven and Hefferin, 1998, 14). Moreover, in another survey, 98 percent of the 737 CEOs interviewed said they would hire someone with a sense of humor over someone with similar qualifications and no sense of humor (Culberson 2000). The bottom line is that leaders of major business organizations overwhelmingly prefer to have leaders with a sense of humor.

Humor cannot only become part of the organizational culture but it can also develop the culture of an organization. Therefore, if you want to help improve the culture within a school or organization, one way to do it is through the use of humor. Take Steve Spurrier, the one-time Florida football coach, who told his Gator fans that a fire at Auburn's football dorm had destroyed twenty books: "But the real tragedy was that fifteen hadn't been colored yet." This is the old chicken-and-egg dilemma, which one comes first? Does humor create the culture of the organization or does the organization help to create an atmosphere conducive for humor? The answer may be that they go hand in hand.

Some say that it is the leader who will typically set the culture of an organization. However, because it takes a community to raise a child, it also takes a community to establish culture. Remember, the three Rs in education today are now defined as: Respect for self; Respect for others; Responsibility for all your actions. Consequently, humor can increase the effectiveness of leaders, which snowballs to improve the culture, which in turn makes the leaders more effective, leading to the use of additional humor and creating an even more positive atmosphere (Ziegler, Boardman, and Thomas 1985). Burford (1985) found that principals with a sense of humor play an important part in the school environment, especially in terms of faculty loyalty and perceptions of school effectiveness.

Unfortunately today, many people do not view schools as being overly effective. Educational institutions seem to be the target of the general public. However, it is always interesting to note that every year in a national survey, individuals give a grade of "D" to the public educational system in the United States, but they also give their own schools a mark of an

"A". How can this be? Part of the problem is perception. Most parents believe that if Martians ever came down to Earth to report on the U.S. educational system, they would report back to their leader that a school appears to be where the relatively young go to watch the relatively old work, but only at another district, not their own school.

DIFFERENT REACTIONS TO HUMOR
WITHIN AN ORGANIZATION

Of course, not everyone views or uses humor in the same manner. Males and females react differently to humor. This is an important point to remember for the development of the culture in the organization. When males are confronted with aggressive behavior, they typically react with aggressive retaliation. Females are most effective in reducing aggression when they react in a friendly manner. It is even known that women and men listen differently. For example, when a man nods his head up and down while listening to someone he is agreeing with what is being said. However, when a woman nods her head up and down, she is indicating that she is listening closely and is hearing everything, but she may or may not agree with what is being said. Consequently, men think women are agreeing with them and will assume a meeting of the minds yet the woman is secretly thinking, "I certainly understand what you are saying but you are completely wrong, you moron."

Here are five observations on how women use humor in the workplace to affect the organizational culture:

1. Humor is used to soften managerial injunctions (directives or orders),
2. Women define humor as fun or lightness,
3. Humor is linked to a sense of appropriateness and a concern for maintaining feminine relational injunctions,
4. Humor works to migrate managerial power interests and to subordinate these interests in favor of relationships,
5. Conversational humor frees middle-management women from the contrary feminine injunctions and privileges managerial injunctions. (Martin 2001)

As we know, all managerial injunctions or directives are not always clear and the organizational culture can both help and hinder the communication of such directions for both men and women. Nevertheless, men find anything funny, especially anything about drinking, sex, and the opponent's losing streak in any sport—for example, my two favorite teams are the Green Bay Packers and anyone playing the Minnesota Vikings.

PRACTICAL POINTS TO PONDER

Bolman and Deal (1997) note in their research that there are four frames of an organization that help define its culture: the political frame, human resources frame, structural frame, and symbolic frame. Here are practical suggestions for leaders to use humor in the four frames to create a more positive culture:

1. Political Frame: Humor has to start at the top. Like any good "initiative," the president, principal, or leader needs to have a sense of humor for him or her to be accepted within an organization. People say that you have to be born with a sense of humor, but this is not an accurate statement. There is no such thing as a person who cannot be funny, only those who are not willing to try.
2. Human Resources Frame: Although you do not have to hire only individuals who have a great sense of humor, review the research data in this chapter. The vast majority of organizations look specifically for leaders with a sense of humor. It helps build culture. Hire the humorous.
3. Structural Frame: Allow humor to flow within an organization. Promote the use of humor in the minutes of meetings and daily activities. Have dress-up days, and allow holidays to be celebrated with ornate costumes, plays, or activities brought forward. This helps make work more fun, and it is also the great equalizer. The principals at many schools have caught on to this fact when they pledge to milk a cow if 100 percent of the third graders reach a reading level or achieve a fund-raising goal.

4. Symbolic Frame:

   a. Allow individuals to decorate their offices anyway they want. I
      work with an advertising agency where they have a Ping-Pong
      table, complete with bleachers, in the middle of their meeting
      room. One staff member has his desk made up to look like the front
      of a car, with a stuffed deer on the floor in front to make it look like
      the "car" has hit the deer. Another individual has his office de-
      signed as a museum with a tag on every item indicating who do-
      nated it and the price tag, including the lamp, desk, chair, and so
      on. This is great for morale and the empowerment of others.

   b. Put humorous signs on doors. Daily cartoons or acceptable draw-
      ings lighten up the atmosphere.

   c. Start meetings out with a joke. Have everyone take turns bringing
      in a new joke to start a class, a meeting, or general group activity.

   d. Have your staff read humorous books that have a message. Books
      like *Leadership Secrets by Attila the Hun* by Wes Roberts (1990)
      can be both clever and informative.

11

Humor and Teamwork, Socialization, and Relationships or Teamwork Is Having Others Do What I Say

LEARNING ORGANIZATIONS

Three of the main components affecting the development of culture within a school or organization are the levels of teamwork, socialization, and relationships. It is almost impossible to define a learning organization in one or two paragraphs, but essentially they emphasize teamwork, strong community relationships, empowerment, consensus, celebration of the learning process, and an environment that is helpful and understanding, even with mistakes being made. Learning organizations are almost utopian in nature, promoting professional development, complete sharing of information, breaking down paradigms, open and free-flowing communication, with an emphasis on total quality management, continuous improvement, socialization, and strong relationships within the community. (Now, how many buzzwords did I hit in this one paragraph?)

Teamwork

At almost every organization, as groups develop, they typically go through the stages of forming, storming, norming, and performing. Others know these stages as groping, griping, grasping, and grouping. In either case, a group typically needs to get oriented and then goes through conflict as it begins to adjust. The group soon becomes organized as self-actualization and cooperation starts to materialize. Joking behavior is characteristic of all work groups and can enhance efficiency and effectiveness. For the members of the group to effectively navigate through the four stages of group development, joking behavior helps maintain balance while building camaraderie. Humor within an activity brings people together and can influence the social climate of the small group and then consequently affect an entire organization (Banning and Nelson 1987).

Listed here are several guidelines for effectively matching management humor and selected individuals or group characteristics:

1. Humor is an aspect of attitudes and personality that should be used by leaders at all levels.
2. Potentially offensive effects of joking behavior can be minimized by creating an environment based on trust. The more that humor can become personalized, the stronger the group will become, and the faster the relationships within that group will move forward.
3. Aggressive and put-down humor should not be used.
4. Leaders need to encourage a climate of reciprocal humor, so upper management is not the only group allowed to use it.
5. Humor should recognize the dignity of all individuals, while demonstrating that employees can place confidence in the leader's objectivity and appropriate sense of justice (Duncan 1982, 140–41).

For individuals to be members of the group or team at work, they need to develop attributes of a family. Interestingly, families that are categorized as strong are typically found to use more wit, jokes, and family fun than those families categorized to be weak (Wuerffel, DeFrain, and Stinnett 1990).

In the same vein, humor promotes group unity, relieves tension, and stimulates creative thinking. These activities lead to a better work environment and more socialization with staff and customers or clients (Pease 1991). Others agree that humor can reduce tension, increase motivation, aid instruction, strengthen teacher-student relationships, and help behavior management—walk on water, do the laundry, etc. (Rareshide 1993). Nevertheless, this all adds up to the fact that humor helps build cooperation and teamwork.

At one point during a game, the coach called one of his seven year-old baseball players aside and asked, "Do you understand what cooperation is? What teamwork is?" The little boy nodded in the affirmative. "Do you understand that what matters is whether we win or lose together as a team?" The little boy nodded yes.

"So," the coach continued, "I'm sure you know, when an out is called, you shouldn't argue, curse, attack the umpire, throw dirt in his face, or call him names. Do you understand all that?" Again, the little boy nodded.

He continued, "And when I take you out of the game so another boy gets a chance to play, it's not good sportsmanship to call your coach dumb, is it?" Again the little boy nodded.

"Good," said the coach. "Now go over there and explain all that to your mother."

Humor and Socialization and Relationships

Humor also has a direct affect on the socialization of employees in the work environment, which is also interrelated to the relationships within a school or organization. Researchers over the years have found that a high sense of humor facilitated the reduction of uncertainty and also served to reduce social distance between interactants. There can be dozens of positive effects of humor and its role in communication, interpersonal relationships, on small groups, and in organizational environments (Curtis and Hansen 1990).

Because of the class structure in most schools and organizations, the use of humor for socialization and relationship building has interesting parameters. Just like every person has an individual style of humor, or no sense of humor, every organization is unique. Humor may be able to affect group dynamics and the organizational culture in a positive way, but the opposite is also true. If you work in a school or organization that does not appreciate humor, you have limited options. You can try to change the culture, live with it, or find a new job.

The other parameter guiding humor, socialization, and relationships is the pure hierarchical nature of most organizations. Research has shown that leaders in positions of authority have more freedom to initiate humor than employees further down the organizational structure (Duncan 1982). Lower-status employees probably need the use of humor more than individuals in higher (and "safer") positions. This means that students typically get to use humor less frequently than teachers. Individuals in authority positions need to be aware of the situation to provide a safe environment for learning and humor. Leaders should allow humor to be used by everyone, and not be limited by position or authority.

If your boss or teacher does not appreciate or use humor, then the odds of you being able to use humor are greatly diminished. Therefore, in order for a group, department, or school to be accepting of humor, it must start at the top. Just like any change initiative, the top administration must provide conscious approval to be successful. This does not mean that humor cannot be used without a memo from the president or superintendent, but it probably means that humor will be limited in its scope to your own smaller group of friends or colleagues.

In addition, every organization or school has certain cultural guidelines that must be respected. For example, as noted previously, one does not tell jokes that are derogatory against the Green Bay Packers. (I actually think that it should be a law not to make any jokes about the Packers in the United States.) The same is true for not joking about the mission of a school or the reverence of the culture, history, and taboos within the organization or school.

Humorous behavior and "getting the joke" can be a source of validation and solidarity with people within the culture. Being accepted as one of the group that takes part in the joking around provides an invitation to an insider, facilitates ties to informal leaders, and makes work more rewarding and enjoyable (Eastmond 1992).

To demonstrate these points, in 1985, Virginia Ziegler, Gerald Boardman, and M. Donald Thomas found in their research with a 0.05 level of significance that there was a:

1. significant positive correlation between neat, lighthearted humor and the leadership factor; and
2. significant negative correlation between dullness humor and the leadership factor.

Now, I am not really sure how you can be quantify the relationships to within a 95-percent level of confidence, but the conclusions are supported by others and also support my main theme, so they are going to be used.

Listed are a few of my own related findings that may help you develop your own leadership factor:

1. Managers do the right thing, and leaders do things right.
2. You can always count on leaders to do the right thing after trying everything else. (This applies even more specifically to technology departments.)
3. Hark, there goes the crowd! I must hurry because I am their leader.
4. The squeeze is more important than the juice.
5. If everyone is complaining and you are the fire hydrant, don't worry, because at least you have all of the dogs together.
6. A leader is a person who knows when to hold someone up and when to push him or her down the stairs.
7. Many organizations are too political with everyone climbing up the ladder. At my organization, we do not even have a ladder.

PRACTICAL POINTS TO PONDER

Here are a few ways to use humor in leadership positions:

1. Use humorous illustrations in presentations and meetings.
2. Videotape clever TV ads to be used as visual aids and inspiration.
3. Use cartoons that support your ideas.
4. Develop patterns of humor at work, for example, running gags.
5. Find one person to be the good humor man/woman. Look for him or her to supply humor, but establish rapport so this person can be "picked on."
6. Provide a positive reinforcement for using humor—for example, compliments, candy, and so on.

12

Humor and Change or
I'll Change When Hell Freezes Over

The only ones who really like change are those initiating the change and babies with wet diapers. However, change is essential in today's environment, both for individuals and for organizations. Michael Burger (n d), a humor specialist, notes that humor can get people more receptive to change by having them open up, become more relaxed, and be accepting of new ideas.

TRAILBLAZERS MODEL

In the twenty-first century, there will be two different kinds of organizations: those that change and those that cease to exist. Nevertheless, many individuals are reluctant to do things differently. Phillip Schlechty (1998), an organizational expert, writes about the trailblazers model of change. He purports that there are five different types of individuals in an organization: trailblazers, pioneers, settlers, stay-at-homers, and saboteurs. Trailblazers are those people who are out in front promoting change. They may not be successful, but they pave the way for others. Pioneers follow the trailblazers and are the ones who are innovative and start the change process. Settlers are typically the largest group within an organization; they accept change with the right direction and information. However, this is the group that needs to be convinced of the importance of change. The stay-at-homers resist change, but could come around with a great deal of convincing. And finally, the saboteurs are not only resistant to change, they attempt to sabotage the process.

In the trailblazers model, all five groups need to be addressed while promoting change, and they must also be considered when using humor. Just like the trailblazer model, different people use humor in different fashions. There are the trailblazers who try using humor, and do not care what others think. There are those who take the lead in using humor, others who follow the lead, and even those who will not use humor no matter what. Others may even sabotage your attempts at humor. Research shows that the most creative people are the ones who tend to laugh the most and vice versa. The idea is to be a trailblazer, while getting the pioneers and settlers to use humor. Just be careful with the saboteurs.

Individuals who have a better sense of humor typically are also more accepting of change. Moreover, organizations that have a culture promoting humor will also accept change more readily. Several of the studies conducted in recent years have found that humor, change, creativity, and cognition were all closely related (Duncan 1984; Duncan and Feisal 1989; Kushner 1990; Hughes, Ginnett, and Curphy 1995). Although humor will not make change happen, it can help with the process. If nothing else, humor can make change a little more fun, and build enthusiasm. Winston Churchill once said, "Success is going from failure to failure without a loss of enthusiasm."

Humor is a major ingredient for organizational change because it helps with creativity, encourages relaxation, enhances attention, and helps with positive attitudes, team building, and interpersonal relationships (Lane 1993). This is quite a mouthful, even if many bosses today believe that "Teamwork is a lot of people doing what I say." Humor also helps with the organizational change process by reducing stress (Osif and Harwood 2000). Change is almost always a difficult and stressful time, so the free use of humor can be a cathartic method of releasing anxiety or built-up stress.

Change is typically associated with unrest and confusion prior to some sort of new structure. A famous author accurately depicted the disorder associated with new ideas when Dr. Seuss wrote *The Cat in the Hat* (55):

> But your mother will come,
> She will find this big mess!
> And this mess is so big
> And so deep and so tall
> We can not pick it up
> There is no way at all!

We all know that the Cat in the Hat made it through successfully. Using quotes from Dr. Seuss and other well-known children books is a humorous and clever way to help make your points. People relate to Dr. Seuss or Sesame Street and feel "safe" when hearing the words. Consequently, it makes them smile and they may be a little more open to hearing about change. I have a full library of Dr. Seuss and other children's books to use for quotes.

As noted, change can be hard to come by, even if what is currently being done makes no sense. Some people do not like change because of the unknown. Therefore, by using quotes from Dr. Seuss, or recognizable and comfortable stories, individuals will start feeling more secure in the change process. Here is a great story to use when introducing change.

Once upon a time there was a cage containing five monkeys. Inside the cage hung a banana on a string and a set of stairs under it. Before long, a monkey would climb the stairs towards the banana. As soon as he touched the stairs, the other monkeys got sprayed with cold water. After a while, another monkey made an attempt with the same result—all the other monkeys were sprayed with cold water. Pretty soon, when another monkey tried to climb the stairs, the other monkeys would prevent it. Now, put away the cold water. Remove one monkey from the cage and replace it with a new one. The new monkey sees the banana and tries to climb the stairs. To his surprise and horror, all of the other monkeys attack him. After another attempt and attack, he knows that if he tries to climb the stairs, he will be assaulted. Next, remove another of the original five monkeys and replace it with a new one. The newcomer goes to the stairs and is attacked. The previous newcomer takes part in the punishment with enthusiasm! Likewise, replace a third original monkey with a new one, then a fourth, then the fifth. Every time the newest monkey takes to the stairs, he is attacked. Most of the monkeys that are beating him have no idea why they were not permitted to climb the stairs or why they are participating in the beating of the newest monkey. After replacing all the original monkeys, none of the remaining monkeys have ever been sprayed with cold water. Nevertheless, no monkey ever again approaches the stairs to try for the banana. Why not? Because as far as they know, that is the way it's always been done around here. That is how company policy begins.

Leaders change, organizations change, and humor changes over time. In the twenty-first century, the factory of the future will have two employees: one person and one dog. The person will be there to feed the dog. The dog will be there to keep the person away from the technology.

Organizations need humor just to help people make sense out of often-confusing activities. Consequently, many offices have even developed their own language to try to make sense out of confusing, or changing situations. Listed here are some of the new office terms for the twenty-first century that may help new leaders.

1. 404—Someone who's clueless. From the World Wide Web error message "404 Not Found," meaning that the requested document could not be located. "Don't bother asking him. . . . He's 404, man."
2. Adminisphere—The rarefied organizational layers beginning just above the rank and file. Decisions that fall from the adminisphere are often profoundly inappropriate or irrelevant to the problems they were designed to solve.
3. Blamestorming—Sitting around in a group discussing why a deadline was missed or a project failed and who was responsible.
4. CLM (Career-Limiting Move)—Used among microserfs to describe ill-advised activity. Trashing your boss while he or she is within earshot is a serious CLM. (Also known as *CEB—Career-Ending Behavior*.)
5. Dilberted—To be exploited and oppressed by your boss. Derived from the experiences of Dilbert, the comic-strip engineer in the job from hell. "I've been dilberted again. The old man revised the specs for the fourth time this week."
6. Ohnosecond—That minuscule fraction of time in which you realize that you've just made a *big* mistake. (See CLM.)
7. Percussive Maintenance—The fine art of whacking an electronic device—just right—to get it to work again.

8. Prairie Dogging—When someone yells or drops something loudly in a "cube farm" (an office full of cubicles) and everyone's heads pop up over the walls to see what's going on.
9. Salmon Week—The experience of spending an entire week swimming upstream only to die, and someone else gets the benefit.
10. Seagull Manager—A manager who flies in, makes a lot of noise, poops on everything, and then leaves.
11. Tourists—People who take training classes just to get a vacation from their jobs. "We had three serious students in the class; the rest were just tourists."
12. Treeware—Printed computer software/hardware documentation.

Statistical analysis has even been used to find the relationship of humor to the change in learning. Gruner (1978) used an analysis of variance with "funniness ratings" correlating the effect of humor on and results of verbal SAT scores. I would go more into this study, but you know the old saying, statistics are like bikinis: What you see is interesting, but what they are hiding is even more interesting. Suffice it to say that humor and SAT scores have a positive correlation.

PRACTICAL POINTS TO PONDER

1. When you are hiring for your office or organization, look for individuals who have a sense of humor. They will tend to be more creative and apt to accept change.
2. Bring in a comedian or improvisational troupe as part of professional development. This type of "training" will not only add to the culture of the organization but it sends a strong message that humor is not only acceptable but almost required.
3. Develop humor policies. The rules can be used to set guidelines for groups to help prevent outrageous behavior, but it also helps to establish a culture of humor.
4. As a leader, try to joke equally with everyone. If you have a favorite person to joke around with, it will be viewed as favoritism. By including everyone, a broader and deeper culture will be developed within the organization.
5. Laugh at yourself when you make mistakes.

13

Humor and the Relationship to Emotions, Stress, and Anxiety or What Do You Really Mean by That?

The strong desire for superiority, the need to be "in" on the joke, the release of tension, and the need to better understand the psychology and the relationships within an organization are important tools for leaders. Organizations like Safeway, the IRS, and Northwestern Bell have all started using humor training to help with the rising costs of health care. All three organizations integrate service and humor in the training sessions. (Think about it . . . the IRS uses humor training.) Organizations also use humor to help leaders get problems under control by allowing for the release of stress (Winnick 1976). As noted previously, the correct use of humor takes training and practice, like any other skill set. Quality leaders are able to tell someone to go to hell so well that they look forward to the journey. This expression may not fit here, but I needed to get it into the book and I was running out of time. In other words, the stress was mounting and now I took care of it. Point proven.

By using humor in the workplace, leaders are able to build relationships, create a more positive work environment, reduce stress, and motivate employees (Sinha and Misra 1960). In addition, it is interesting to note that humor has even been positively correlated with financial bonuses and the self-confidence of executives (Sinha and Misra 1960). Trust me, if I got a huge bonus, I would have more confidence and a better sense of humor, too.

Daily activities can be as stressful, and sometimes even more stressful, than crisis situations. One way to address this concern is to give humorous awards to employees. The awards can be funny and even send meaningful messages. Of course, some employees are already motivated and do not need any help from management:

> The owner of a Guinness factory goes to the home of one of his workers. He says to the woman who answers the door, "Mary, I have some terrible news for you. Your husband John died today at work." Mary cries, "How did this happen?" The owner says, "He fell into a vat of Guinness and drowned." Mary says, "I hope at least he went fast." The owner says, "Sorry, but this was not the case. He got out of the vat three times to go to the bathroom."

THE *BIG* QUESTION

To be (humorous) or not to be (humorous), that is the question. Some leaders may argue that humor does not work nor does it relieve the stress of the day. Here is the bottom line: If there is nothing to lose, then why not try it? It is similar to the theory of Blaise Pascal (1623–1662) who was a pioneer in mathematical probability and gambling. "But either God exists or he does not exist, and we are unable to tell which alternative is true. However, both our present lives and our possible future lives may well be greatly affected by the alternative we accept." Pascal argued that because eternal happiness is the ultimate goal "(if God does exist) and nothing is lost if we are wrong about the other choice (if God does not exist and we choose to believe that he does), the reasonable gamble, given what may be at stake, is to choose the theistic alternative. He who remains an unbeliever is taking an infinitely unreasonable risk just because he does not know which alternative is true" (Pascal, quoted in Popkin 1967).

The gamble here is not a gamble at all. If you use humor and it relieves stress and anxiety, then it is a win-win proposition. If you use humor but it does not relieve the stress and anxiety at work, no harm, no foul—at least your staff thinks you are funny and your popularity increases (Gruner 1965). Leaders like nothing more than being appreciated, and they need to know the psychology behind humor to use it more efficiently.

PRACTICAL POINTS TO PONDER

Putting the information together on psychology, stress, and anxiety, here are a few observations concerning school leaders and humor.

1. Leaders who use humor can help teachers and staff work more closely together, thereby reducing stress and increasing the efficiency of an organization. There are three kinds of people in the world today: 1) Those who make things happen, 2) those who watch things happen, and 3) those who wonder what happened. Courage separates the three. Students and staff will emulate behavior you model. Use clever sayings in daily conversations.

2. Leaders who use humor feel more in tune with the staff.

> The Americans and the Japanese decided to engage in a competitive boat race. Both teams practiced hard and long to reach their peak performance. On the big day both felt ready. The Japanese won by a mile. Afterward, the American team was discouraged. Corporate management hired a consulting firm to investigate the problem and recommended corrective action. After a year of study and millions spent analyzing the problem, the consultant firm concluded that too many people were steering and not enough were rowing. The Japanese team had eight people rowing and one person steering; the American team had one person rowing and eight people steering. So as race day neared the following year, the American team's management structure was completely reorganized. The new structure consisted of four steering managers, three area steering managers, and a new performance review system for the one person rowing. The next year, the Japanese won by two miles. Humiliated, the American corporation laid off the rower for poor performance and gave the managers a bonus for discovering the problem.

   Do not lay off the rower. Use stories in the context of explanations and to problem-solve.

3. Leaders who use humor seem more part of the group, more accessible, and approachable.

   Start slowly by interjecting humor in the classroom, meetings, or functions. People do not think that they can be funny, but it is like learning how to golf. You might never be a professional golfer, but you can certainly learn the rules of the game and have fun. Take it slow, read up on the topic, and practice, practice, practice.

> The Marx Brothers were making a movie in the 1950s that contained a scene in which they were playing bridge. In order to add realism to the scene, the director brought in a bridge expert to teach the Marx Brothers how to play. On the first day, the bridge expert started out by explaining that bridge is played with one deck of cards, and sometimes two decks. Groucho jumped on the table and said, "That's about all we can handle for one day."

4. Leaders who use humor can create a more positive school culture and environment.

> One day a farmer's donkey fell into a deep well. The farmer was devastated because he realized that he could not get the donkey out so he decided to simply fill in the well and buy a new donkey. The farmer got some neighbors together to help and they started to throw shovels of dirt on the donkey, but as they threw dirt into the well, the donkey simply shook it off and stepped up. This process continued for some time and with each new shovel of dirt thrown into the well, the donkey shook it off his back and stepped on top of the new ground. Within a short time, the neighbors had thrown in enough dirt for the donkey to simply walk out of the well. Leadership is not what happens but how secure you are in the reaction to the situation.

5. Leaders who use humor enhance the interpersonal interaction between the administration, teachers, and staff.

> In the summer of 2003, Grace passed away after ninety-seven years of living a full life. Grace moved on to heaven under her own terms and on her own timetable, which is the only way she would do anything. She was the matriarch of the family and took her job seriously. In fact, Grace was a very religious woman of many talents, not the least of which was being a great cook. She made the best baked beans in the world and everyone always asked her for the recipe, to which she would reply, "You may only have the recipe when I die and no sooner." She meant it. As the years wore on, Grace started growing

weaker, so she began to let everyone know that her time had come and she started telling everyone what to do. She informed her son, Jack, that the time had come to pass the recipe on for her baked beans. And she meant it. Grace asked the family members to give the recipe to all of their own friends to share a little happiness at a time of some sorrow. Grace believed that this recipe helped keep the family close because it symbolized the rich traditions that are unique and celebrated by close families. Moreover, the "secret" recipe served to be a family joke for many years. When Grace died, the baked beans recipe was put in the funeral announcement and subsequently passed on to many friends that summer in hopes that it would bring a little joy into the lives of others.

Bring a little joy into the classroom, meeting, or work environment. Ask individuals for similar stories about their families, like the one above. Are there any holiday traditions that may seem unusual to outsiders? Is there an eccentric in your family whom you love but who may do things differently? Asking these questions can be done in a playful manner that will bring individuals closer together and make the leader one of the group.

6. Leaders who use humor make work more enjoyable and positive (Marken 1999).

Instead of having an employee of the month, give an award to the Humorous Employee of the Month. This can also be adjusted to be an award in class or at a meeting for the best joke, most original expression, and so on. A piece of candy or standing ovation can be the reward. At our meetings, I identify the "Idea of the Month." If someone presents a great idea, I indicate that it was, in fact, a great idea, and let them know that they are now "done thinking" for the month. This is a running joke with the staff and everyone gets involved. They even fight over whether it was good enough for the "reward."

14

Humorous Organizations or My School Is a Joke

If you work in education, then you certainly are familiar with the work of Peter Senge. And if you do not know his work, you fake it at the faculty cocktail parties. By the way do you know where the word *cocktail* comes from? Back around the Civil War, Southerners who owned large planta- tions would celebrate the end of the growing season with several weeks of parties after all of the crops were collected. Typically, the owners would try to outdo one another with extravagant festivities. One of the main at- tractions would be to decorate the various drinks with feathers from birds and one of the most colorful was the cock tail feather, hence the name *cocktail party*. Once again, my history major comes through.

Humor is a universally accepted concept and provides another tool in your leadership arsenal. You can lead a horse to water, but you cannot make him drink. (Another free expression for you to use.) Just like in schools, you cannot force students to learn, but you can establish an envi- ronment that fosters academic achievement. Humor also creates a more relaxed environment, with universal appeal.

Senge (1990) has his learning organizations, but funny leaders also have their humorous organizations. Listed are the five areas necessary for a learning organization, as listed by Senge in *The Fifth Discipline*, along with the associated elements of a humorous organization:

1. Systems Thinking: While Senge writes that individuals need to think in terms of systems instead of separate entities, the same is true for

humor. Senge writes, "The essence of the discipline of systems think-ing lies in a shift of mind: 1) seeing interrelationships rather than lin-ear cause-effect chains, and 2) seeing processes of change rather than snapshots" (Senge, Ross, Smith, Roberts, and Kleiner 1994, 73).

Do not just tell a joke to get a cheap laugh, but try to understand the content, frame of reference, and possible consequences of the communication. Humor should not be a separate entity within an or-ganization, but should be integrated into the daily activities. This will not only help to define and develop the culture but will also be symbolic for the organization. For example, individuals who simply tell off-color jokes around the water cooler (if there is such a thing anymore) are sending a much different message than a leader who uses humor to try to teach new material. After all, education is full of magical things waiting for wits to grow sharper.

2. Personal Mastery: Once again, do not just simply tell a joke, but be sure that you know why you are telling the particular joke (have a specific point), anticipate the reactions, and study the theoretical as-pects of humor. Of course, humor should not be so complex as set-ting the VCR, but you do not want to misuse humor and offend any-one. This means that as a leader you need to read about humor, study it, and even make it part of your research when developing leader-ship activities or training. Leaders need to use humor themselves, but also empower employees and allow them to create and explore new ways of using humor.

3. Mental Models: A mental model of humor should challenge employ-ees to find new, better methods to perform a task. Develop a mental model of how you want humor to work and how you expect it to af-fect your leadership. Humor is just like any other leadership device: You cannot simply use it sporadically, without training, or without knowing why it is being used. Your humor model should be developed over time. Will you use it solely as a communication tool, or to psy-chologically affect colleagues? Set your goals high because "What we obtain too cheaply, we esteem too lightly" (Thomas Paine).

Here is my mental model of humor. I call it, "just Jack."

Just do it.

Always look for humorous material to use.

Create an atmosphere of acceptance for humor.

Keep an organized file (database) of material.

I actually have a complete Access database of jokes (hard to tell by this book), organized by topic, where I record the responses for each of the jokes.

4. Building Shared Vision: Building a shared vision for humor is not something that needs to be accomplished through a detailed strategic planning session, but rather can be developed through modeling from the leader. Allow humor to become part of the organization and encourage its use. Like anything else that is positive within a school organization, humor should be encouraged with generally accepted limits or guidelines. Again, this does not have to be completed through a two-year planning process on humor, although this may be fun. (I could just see someone submitting a purchase order to the chief financial officer for a two-day retreat on humor.) However, people should share a common mental model of humor. The culture, mores, and beliefs of the organization will help set the limits.

5. Team Learning: Team learning can be very contagious, so groups learning humor can also be contagious. Researchers found that kids under the age of five laugh 350 times per day, while people over thirty-five laugh five times per day. (I know one vice president who laughs minus five times per day.) Why should the kids have all the fun? Humor develops teamwork, the teams become close and joke around more, which becomes infectious within the organization, and very soon the culture of the organization or school has changed. Humor can be learned and, therefore, it can be used to enhance the culture of an organization and transform it into a less stressful environment by building a bond between individuals and teams, thereby establishing a work environment that is more comfortable and satisfying. When there is a silly play to perform at a holiday celebration, aren't you more apt to participate in a group as opposed to going solo? You will always do foolish things in life, so do them with enthusiasm.

Remember:

- Humor without content is just funny.
- Content without humor is just boring.
- Humor with content is still boring but at least the time passes quickly. (Just kidding, humor with content builds culture.)

CAUTIONS

Like using hazardous material, using humor should come with a few
warnings and cautions that need to be addressed before trying to be funny
without a net:

1. Humor should not be avoided, simply approach it with respect.
2. Minimize the offensive nature of joking by avoiding jokes that dis-
   criminate against people (but not lawyers).
3. Aggressive, put-down humor should generally be avoided.
4. A climate of reciprocal humor should be encouraged.
5. Keep the humor relevant to the situation/context.
6. Be sure that the humor reflects the interests and language of the followers.
7. Make the humor brief and conversational; no one likes to get lost
   in a joke or story and miss the punch line.
8. If delivered in address form, humor must be adapted to a conversational tone not a written tone.
9. Use self-effacing humor if the situation warrants it or if you have
   high credibility.
10. Take your message seriously, but don't take yourself too seriously.
11. Remember to attack the position through humor, not the person's
    dignity.
12. Avoid inconsistent humor; it's better that people think that you
    have no sense of humor than to attack them or not have them un-
    derstand your line of reasoning.
13. Avoid topics that center on sex, illegal activity, or other organiza-
    tional topics that are taboo.
14. Look spontaneous; be prepared.
15. A modicum of apt, relevant humor in informative discourse will
    probably produce a more favorable reaction toward the speaker
    (Gruner 1970).
16. Humor that is self-disparaging may further enhance the image of
    the speaker (Chang and Gruner 1981).
17. Apt, relevant humor can enhance interest in the leader (Gruner 1970).
18. Apt, relevant humor seems not to influence the effectiveness of
    persuasive speeches negatively or positively (Gruner 1985).
19. Humor may make a speech more "memorable" (Taylor 1974).

20. The use of satire as a persuasive device may have unpredictable results (Miller and Bacon 1975, as cited in Alena Group, 2003).

George Will once wrote that, "It is easy to be a humorist when you have the government working for you everyday"

THE BIG PICTURE

Let's face it, you do not become a leader on your first try, nor is there only one fairway to follow to the leadership pinnacle (I am going to see how many golf puns I can squeeze into this section). At times, individuals are able to lead and other times you will miss the cut. Deal with it. Leaders need to be agile, able, and willing to change clubs as they play the game. Everyone experiences highs or lows, and overcomes handicaps throughout his or her career. Humor just may help individuals through it all. As Jack Nicklaus once said, "Never get too high on the victories or too low on the defeats." And remember, practice does not make perfect. Nothing is perfect. Practice simply makes things better.

ONE ANALOGY AFTER ANOTHER OR
HOW DOES IT ALL WORK TOGETHER?

Suggestion #1: Use Different Routes

There is no one right path for an individual using humor as a tool in leadership. Everyone takes a different route, and you can take any path that works best for you. However, it is best to take one step at a time and learn the fundamentals of leadership, learning, and humor before moving on. You do not have to memorize every aspect of humor before moving on, because the idea is that you will return to the basics over and over again as new situations arise.

Suggestion #2: Any Path Works

People are always trying to find the shortcut to leadership with do-it-yourself help books. However, all of the fads are like diet books: They may look good on paper but good old-fashioned hard work is the only way to be successful. Just do it—because there are no shortcuts to leadership or to using humor in leadership. It takes hard work and dedication. The ideal is to implement certain aspects as you progress so that trial and error by practical components is utilized. See suggestion #3.

Suggestion #3: Make Mistakes

In the United States we tend to view mistakes as a sign of weakness, yet leaders are the ones forging new ground and most certainly will make errors. Nevertheless, true leaders are not only servants to others, they also serve by trying something new and by being the trailblazers. They are not afraid of making mistakes. Have you ever been "should on"? This is when someone tells you that you "should have" done this or you "should have" done that. However, it does not matter because "getting knocked down" is a good way to learn how to stand.

Suggestion #4: Remember Where You Have Been

Be sure to remember and respect the past. In this way, you will be able to learn and analyze what works in leadership, learning, and humor, and what does not. Continue to make connections. This is how the brain works and how we continue to analyze and then synthesize new information. Mistakes may be one way to learn, but do not make the same mistake twice. Fool me once, shame on you; fool me twice, shame on me.

Suggestion #5: You Are Only as Good as Your Last Act or as Funny as Your Last Joke

People have short memories. They tend to remember the mistakes just a little longer than the good that we do. Be persistent and never give up. True leaders continue to learn and continue to try to help others. Having someone push you as a leader, or question the decisions, makes us all honest and makes us think about the consequences of our actions. Simply having a "yes" man or woman does no one any good, except maybe your spouse.

Suggestion #6: Always Return to the Fundamentals

What does not kill you makes you stronger. Returning to the fundamentals is another way to become a stronger leader and integrate humor. This means learning more about leadership, learning more and more about humor, continuing to make connections, trying new things, and just seeing what works and what does not work. Life is a marathon, not a 100-meter race; the best way to finish a marathon is through training. The best teachers I know are the ones who continue to learn from their students. "This idea is so important we cannot let things more important interfere with it." (This is actually a quote from a company on an "important" project.) See what I mean that humor is everywhere—even when people are not trying to be funny?

Now that you have all of the information, the rest is up to you. Do not let this become just another fad where you read a book or go to a conference, get all excited for about two weeks, and then allow the enthusiasm to die off. Make the world a better place by developing leadership skills. Transform yourself and organizations by continuing to climb the steps of leadership, learning, and humor to help one another, or at least do not push them down the stairs. If nothing else, use a little humor every day to make the world a little better place to live.

THE FINAL WORD

And now for the pièce de résistance. Deming has his fourteen points, Senge has his learning organization, Bloom has his taxonomy, and now Jonas has his ten laws of humor:

1. *Develop a database of jokes, stories, sayings, and so on.* Every time you go to a conference, hear a speech, or even watch TV, take notes and be sure to add the stories to your database. Be religious about this activity and categorize information for easy use. With modern technology, there are 101 ways to do this from using a PDA to even using cell phones. You can even leave yourself phone messages about a joke or story that you hear so you can put it into the file later on.

2. *You do not have to reinvent the wheel.* Search the Internet and read great books (like this one) to get fresh material. Or just borrow the information. One of the goals of this book is to provide you with jokes, stories, and other material embedded in the text.

3. *Always look for connections with your material.* Do not just cut out a cute cartoon or funny joke. Write a short note on the back where it may fit in with your material or activities. You will be so grateful later on.

4. *As you complete a lesson plan, an organizational meeting, or activity as a leader, be sure to plan out the jokes, stories, humorous overheads, and so forth.* As noted previously, look spontaneous and be prepared. Humor can be learned and planned, it does not have to be extemporaneous. I actually outline my lectures and write in the jokes in the proper places where they should work the best. This one sentence will probably crush all of my students who are still trying to figure out how this may be true when they do not think I am the least bit funny.

5. *Collect overheads and be sure to label them or categorize them.* Share jokes and cartoons with your colleagues. The overhead is a great way to make a point, get someone's attention, and to leave a visual impact on a class. Remember the one = bun, two = shoe exercise. Keep a three-ring binder of overheads and carry them to class, just in case. In fact, there are three questions that you can get from students: good questions, great questions, and excellent questions. Good questions are the ones that you do not know the answer to so you make up something to stall while you think of a good response, like explaining there are three different kinds of questions. Great questions are the ones that you know the answer to. And excellent questions are the ones that you know the answer to and have an overhead to demonstrate. Be prepared.

6. *Track the reactions you get with various jokes, stories, and activities.* This will take some work, but any improvement takes time. Of course, go ahead and reuse the jokes that work and do not be afraid to eliminate the ones that don't, even if you think they are funny.

7. *Look at reality for some of the funniest things to discuss and use.* Students love to learn more about practical aspects of the theoreti-

cal knowledge, and they certainly will be able to make more connections between humor and knowledge from real-life situations (more brain stuff).

8. *Do not be afraid to encourage students to develop a sense of humor in class.* Humor can be very contagious; let it happen. This will mean letting go of some power of being a teacher, but will be worth the effort. Let students tell jokes in class. Let your staff tell jokes.

9. *Just do it.* (I think that I owe Nike some money for using this phrase.) Don't be afraid to make mistakes and look less than perfect. Staff and students will respect you for the chances you take, for your knowledge and sense of humor, if not for your wardrobe.

10. *Be sure that you have tenure before you try any of the suggestions in this book, or at least a second career to fall back on.*

THE FINAL, FINAL WORD

Here is the final story and lessons to be learned.

Question #1: How do you get a giraffe in the refrigerator?

Answer: Open refrigerator, put in giraffe.

Lesson: Do not make the integration of leadership, learning, and humor overly complicated. Keep it simple.

Question #2: How do you get an elephant in the refrigerator?

Wrong Answer: Open the refrigerator and put in the elephant.

Correct Answer: Open refrigerator, take out the giraffe, and put in the elephant.

Lesson: Think through the repercussions of your actions. Do not just tell a joke: Plan for it and think about the consequences of your humor.

Question #3: The Lion King is hosting an animal conference, and all but one animal goes to the conference, which one did not come?

Answer: The elephant did not come because he is in the refrigerator.

Lesson: This question tests your memory. Do not forget what you did in the past, what works, and what does not work. Remember to make humor part of your everyday activities.

Question #4: There is a river you must cross but it is inhabited by crocodiles. How do you get across?

Answer: Just swim—all of the crocodiles are at the Lion King's conference.

Lesson: This particular question tests whether you learn quickly from your mistakes. The same thing is true for humor. Do it. Make mistakes, learn, and move on. And always, always remember to have fun.

A

Interesting Sayings

1. Do not walk behind me, for I might not lead. Do not walk ahead of me, for I might not follow. Do not walk beside me, either. Just leave me alone.
2. The journey of a thousand miles begins with a broken fan belt and a leaky tire.
3. It's always darkest before dawn. So if you're going to steal the neighbor's newspaper, that's the time to do it.
4. It's a small world. So you gotta use your elbows a lot.
5. We are born naked, wet, and hungry. Then things get worse.
6. Always remember you're unique, just like everyone else.
7. Never test the depth of the water with both feet.
8. It might be that your sole purpose in life is simply to serve as a warning to others.
9. It is far more impressive when others discover your good qualities without your help.
10. If you think nobody cares if you're alive, try missing a couple of car payments.
11. If you tell the truth you don't have to remember anything.
12. If you lend someone $20, and never see that person again, it was probably worth it.
13. If you haven't had much education, you must use your brain.
14. Never mess up an apology with an excuse.
15. Never underestimate the power of stupid people in large groups.

16. Give a man a fish and he will eat for a day. Teach him how to fish, and he will sit in a boat and drink beer all day.
17. Taxation with representation isn't so hot, either!
18. Some days you are the bug, some days you are the windshield.
19. Don't worry, it only seems kinky the first time.
20. If at first you don't succeed, skydiving is not for you.
21. Never ask a barber if he thinks you need a haircut.
22. Good judgment comes from bad experience, and a lot of that comes from bad judgment.
23. The quickest way to double your money is to fold it in half and put it back in your pocket.
24. Timing has an awful lot to do with the outcome of a rain dance.
25. A closed mouth gathers no foot.
26. Duct tape is like The Force: It has a light side and a dark side and it holds the universe together.
27. Telling a man to go to hell and making him do it are two entirely different propositions.
28. Eagles may soar, but weasels don't get sucked into jet engines.
29. There are two theories to arguing with women. Neither one works.
30. Never miss a good chance to shut up.
31. Generally speaking, you aren't learning much when your mouth is moving.
32. Anything worth taking seriously is worth making fun of.
33. Diplomacy is the art of saying "good doggie" while looking for a bigger stick.
34. Before you criticize someone, you should walk a mile in his shoes. That way, when you criticize him, you're a mile away and you have his shoes.
35. If Barbie is so popular, why do you have to buy her friends?
36. Experience is something you don't get until just after you need it.
37. The problem with the gene pool is that there is no lifeguard.
38. Don't be irreplaceable; if you can't be replaced, you can't be promoted.

B

Stories

There was once an old rabbi whose wisdom and knowledge of the ways of mystery made him the leader of his people in Israel. Whenever the people were threatened with a catastrophe of whatever kind, they went to him with their pleas: "Intercede for us with God to have him spare us again!"

At that, the old rabbi would go into the heart of a dark forest. Once in the sacred place, he would build a special magic fire that only he knew how to build. And once it was burning, the old rabbi would say the words of the sacred prayer that only he knew. Then he would say, "God, I am here in this dark place of mystery, before the magic fire, having said the sacred prayer that you might spare the people." And, as always, God did spare the people.

One day, the old rabbi died. When next the people of Israel were threatened with catastrophe, they went to his chief disciple and asked him to intercede, whereupon he went into the heart of the forest. Once there, he built the magic fire and then said, "God, I am here in this place of mystery before this magic fire that you might spare the people. I do not know the words of the sacred prayer, so my being here in this holy place will have to be enough." And it was. And God spared the people again.

And the disciple died. The next time Israel was threatened, they went to another disciple and asked him to intercede. He went into the dark forest to the special place of mystery, where he knelt and said, "God, here I am in this sacred place that you might spare the people. I know neither how to build the magic fire nor the words of the secret prayer. So my being here in this holy place will have to be enough." And it was. And God spared the people again.

And that disciple died. The next time Israel was threatened with catastrophe, they went to another disciple and asked him to intercede for them with God. Well, he leaned back in the easy chair of his living room resting his head upon his fists. He said, "God, I do not know how to find the holy place in the forest. So my telling you this story will have to be enough." And it was. And God spared the people again because, you see, God created human beings because God loves stories.

COMMUNICATION

Socrates was completely against writing because it was static and non-changing. Instead he argued for a give-and-take exchange of information in order to learn and grow. Writing, he said, is rigid and the antithesis of learning. The written word will only let you follow an argument, not participate in it. He did not put anything in writing. Just as Socrates predicted, memorization of the written word became the sign of intellect. The more you could recite word for word, the greater your intellect. Socrates had a different idea of communication.

COMPETENCE

The noted English architect, Sir Christopher Wren, once built a structure in London. His employers claimed that a certain span Wren planned was too wide and that he would need another row of columns for support. Sir Christopher, after some discussion, acquiesced. He added the row of columns but he left a space between the unnecessary columns and beams above. The public cannot see this space from the ground. To this day, the beam has not sagged. The columns still stand firm, supporting nothing but Wren's conviction and competence.

DISCERNMENT

One day an army sergeant was trying to explain the differences between military training and military education. One of the students in the audience could not get the distinction. So the sergeant said, "Do you have a daughter?" He responded, "Yes, I do." The sergeant then said, "Do you want your daughter learning sex education or sex training?"

FOCUS

Three dogs are sitting in front of a steak house. The first dog said, "I used to be a chef in a previous life and I know how to get a steak." The second dog said, "Wait a minute, I was a lawyer in a previous life and I know how to negotiate for a steak." Finally the third dog said, "That may be true, but I was a college president in a previous life and if the three of us just sit here and whine long enough, someone will bring us a steak." All three dogs were focused on the goal.

GENEROSITY

A young man was getting ready to graduate from college. For many months, he had admired a beautiful sports car in a dealer's showroom, and knowing his father could well afford it, he told him that was all he wanted. Finally, on the morning of his graduation, his father called him into his private study. His father told him how proud he was to have such a fine son, and told him how much he loved him. He handed his son a beautifully wrapped gift box. Curious, but somewhat disappointed, the young man opened the box and found a lovely, leather-bound Bible. Angrily, he raised his voice at his father and said, "With all your money, you give me a Bible?" and stormed out of the house, leaving the holy book. Many years passed and the young man was very successful in business. He had not seen his father since that graduation day. One day, he received a telegram telling him his father had passed away, and willed all of his possessions to his son. When he arrived at his father's house, sudden sadness and regret filled his heart. He began to search through his father's important papers and saw the still unused Bible, just as he had left it years ago. With tears in his eyes, he opened the Bible, and began to turn the pages. As he read the words, a car key dropped from an envelope taped in the back of the Bible. It had a tag with the dealer's name, the same dealer who had the sports car he had desired. On the tag was the date of his graduation, and the words . . . PAID IN FULL. How many times do we miss acts of generosity because they are not packaged as we expected?

PROBLEM SOLVING

You are driving along on a wild stormy night. You pass by a bus stop, and you see three people waiting for the bus:

1. An old lady who is about to die.
2. An old friend who once saved your life.
3. The perfect man (or) woman you have been dreaming about.

Which one would you choose, knowing that there could only be one passenger in your car? This is a moral/ethical dilemma that was once actually used as part of a job application.

You could pick up the old lady, because she is going to die, and thus you should save her first or you could take the old friend because he once saved your life, and this would be the perfect chance to pay him back. However, you may never be able to find your perfect dream lover again.

The correct answer? Give the car keys to the old friend, and let him take the lady to the hospital. Stay behind and wait for the bus with the woman of your dreams. Sometimes, we gain more if we are able to give up our stubborn thought limitations (think "out of the box").

SELF-DISCIPLINE

A man 103 years old was interviewed by a young lady. "To what do you attribute your long life?" Answer: "No drinking or smoking and walking three miles per day." Interviewer: "My mother followed the exact same regimen and died at sixty-eight." The old man said: "I guess she was not self-disciplined to do it long enough."

SERVANTHOOD

Two friends were walking through the desert. During some point of the journey they had an argument, and one friend slapped the other one in the face. The one who got slapped was hurt, but without saying anything, wrote in the sand: "Today my best friend slapped me in the face."

They kept on walking until they found an oasis, where they decided to take a bath. The one who had been slapped got stuck in the mire and started drowning, but the friend saved him. After he recovered from the near drowning, he wrote on a stone: "Today my best friend saved my life."

The friend who had slapped and saved his best friend asked him, "After I hurt you, you wrote in the sand and now, you write on a stone, why?" The other friend replied: "When someone hurts us we should write it down in sand where winds of forgiveness can erase it away. But, when someone does something good for us, we must engrave it in stone where no wind can ever erase it."

C

Lists That Can Be Used by Leaders

OXYMORONS

1. Soft rock
2. Alone together
3. Military intelligence
4. Sweet sorrow
5. Passive aggressive
6. Clearly misunderstood
7. Peace force
8. Plastic glass
9. Act naturally
10. Found missing
11. Good grief
12. Small crowd
13. Extinct life
14. Computer security
15. Definite maybe
16. Exact estimate
17. Pretty ugly
18. Working vacation
19. Religious tolerance
20. Microsoft works

WORLD'S THINNEST BOOKS BY LEADERS

1. *Things I Can't Afford* by Bill Gates
2. *Things I Would Not Do For Money* by Dennis Rodman
3. *The Wild Years* by Al Gore
4. *Amelia Earhart's Guide to the Pacific Ocean*
5. *America's Most Respected Lawyers*
6. *Dr. Kevorkian's Collection of Motivational Speeches*
7. *Everything Men Know about Women*
8. *Everything Women Know about Men*
9. *Mike Tyson's Guide to Dating Etiquette*
10. *Spotted Owl Recipes* by the Sierra Club
11. *The Amish Phone Directory*
12. *My Book of Morals* by Bill Clinton and Gary Condit (with a foreword by Rev. Jesse Jackson).

TWENTY THINGS LEADERS NEED TO KNOW

1. Age is a very high price to pay for maturity.
2. Going to church doesn't make you a Christian any more than standing in a garage makes you a car.
3. Artificial intelligence is no match for natural stupidity.
4. If you must choose between two evils, pick the one you've never tried before.
5. Not one shred of evidence supports the notion that life is serious.
6. It is easier to get forgiveness than permission.
7. For every action, there is an equal and opposite government program.
8. If you look like your passport picture, you probably need the trip.
9. Bills travel through the mail at twice the speed of checks.
10. A conscience is what hurts when all of your other parts feel so good.
11. Men are from Earth. Women are from Earth. Deal with it.
12. No man has ever been shot while doing the dishes.
13. A balanced diet is a cookie in each hand.
14. Middle age is when broadness of the mind and narrowness of the waist change places.
15. Opportunities always look bigger going than coming.

16. Junk is something you've kept for years and throw away three weeks before you need it.
17. There is always one more imbecile than you counted on.
18. Experience is a wonderful thing. It enables you to recognize a mistake when you make it again.
19. By the time you can make ends meet, they move the ends.
20. Someone who thinks logically provides a nice contrast to the real world.

HUMAN TRUTHS

Here is a list of "Human Truths" that a leading public relations firm developed to help them with ad campaigns. They were developed through market research and are real.

1. Most people would switch religions for $10,000.
2. Most people would rather lose their sense of smell than any other.
3. Fifty percent of all women would rather have chocolate than sex.
4. The majority of parents admit to having a favorite child.
5. One out of every twenty expectant fathers mimics symptoms of pregnancy.
6. Babies do not naturally fear darkness, but develop a fear after being put alone to bed.
7. Young, well-educated women get more headaches than any other group.
8. Seventeen percent of all married women know their husbands have been unfaithful.
9. Five women will commit murder today with no regrets.
10. Falling is the most common nightmare.
11. Babies can smile in the womb but must learn to frown at about six months.
12. Women commit one out of ten violent crimes, which are always categorized as a crime of passion.
13. Americans consume five tons of aspirin a day.
14. The vast majority of all women believe all wives lie to their husbands.
15. Most men part their hair to the left for no apparent reason.

16. Most women open their mouths when applying mascara.
17. There has never been a human society that hasn't made up stories.
18. Sixty-seven percent of Americans think they're overweight.
19. Most people believe all politicians will lie to get your vote.
20. Two percent of the population believes the characters played by actors on TV and in movies are real.
21. Most people think they will die in a horrible car accident.
22. More people have a greater fear of spiders than anything else.
23. Most people talk out loud to themselves while alone.
24. Thirty-six percent of all men change jobs every year, 26 percent of all women.
25. Most people feel uncomfortable shaking hands with ministers, priests, or rabbis.
26. Most people admit to imagining coworkers naked.
27. Fifty percent of all people who have borrowed money from friends would rather end the friendship than pay it back.
28. People worry about exceeding the weight limits of elevators yet there has never been an elevator mishap anywhere due to weight.
29. "Mary" has been the most common girl's name for more than a hundred years.
30. Men mistrust police officers more than women; women mistrust hair stylists more than men.
31. The older a man gets, the more dependent he becomes; the older a woman gets, the more independent she becomes.
32. Women think of shoes as reflections of their personalities, men think of shoes as attire.
33. Females hear better than males at every age. Especially married males.
34. Twenty-five percent of all people snoop in friends' medicine cabinets.
35. Eighty percent of all boys would marry one of their elementary school teachers if it was legal.
36. Americans throw away 27 percent of our food each year.
37. Americans spend more on cat food than baby food.
38. The average American will spend two years of his life waiting for meals to be served.
39. Seventy-six percent of teenagers believe in angels.

40. Thirty-eight percent of men say they love their cars more than their women.
41. Thirty percent of all people asked to participate in a poll refuse.
42. Most women believe other women's compliments are insincere.
43. Americans spend about six months of their lives waiting at red lights.
44. Eighty-six percent of all married people admit to giving their spouse the finger when he or she isn't looking.
45. Twenty percent of the people in human history are alive today.
46. Sixty-one percent of college women, but only 28 percent of college men, say they are in a steady relationship.
47. Half of all bank robbers choose Fridays for their crime.
48. Only 15 percent of people bite their fingernails when nervous or anxious.
49. Seventy-five percent of industrial accidents happen to people who skipped breakfast that day.
50. Ninety-four percent of women disk jockeys wear makeup on the radio
51. Most women think facial scars on men are sexy.
52. Fifty-one percent of American men say TV remote controls have significantly increased their quality of life.
53. Eighteen percent of women and 9 percent of men would rather give up sex for a week than their remote control.
54. Sixty-three percent of Americans spend at least five minutes a day looking for their remote.
55. Men leave hotel rooms much cleaner than women, according to maids.
56. Forty-two percent of Americans say they have spent extra time in the bathroom to avoid coworkers.
57. The vast majority of Americans say they're annoyed by advertisements; the vast majority of Europeans say they're entertained by advertisements.
58. Most people dream of one day becoming rich and firing everyone at their place of work.
59. Sixty percent of Americans call their mothers once a week.
60. Twenty-five percent of the people at sporting events believe their presence affects the outcome of the game.

61. Forty percent of American workers describe their boss as "dumb."
62. Twenty-five percent of Americans believe in ghosts.
63. Thirty-one percent of Americans will not watch a film with subtitles no matter how good it is.
64. Sixty-one percent of American workers have napped on the job.
65. The average American mom spends an hour a day behind the wheel of a car.
66. One in twelve men are colorblind, but only one woman in a hundred is.
67. Most girls would rather be spanked by their dads than their moms.
68. Sixty-nine percent of people eat the cake first, then the frosting.
69. Doctors more than any other profession are most likely to be late for a doctor's appointment.
70. Thirty-six percent of people choose pizza for the one food they would eat if they could only eat one.
71. According to women, men can be "too good looking." According to men, women can never be "too good looking."
72. You spend a year of your life looking for misplaced objects.
73. In virtually every species, females outlive males.
74. One out of ten children sleepwalk.
75. Men get hiccups much more often than women, for no known reason.
76. Women find "confidence" the most attractive quality in a man; men find "a good body" the most attractive quality in a woman.
77. People laugh least in the first half hour after waking up.
78. Forty percent of all American couples first discuss marriage in a car.
79. Most men say they are "repulsed" by smelling other men's cologne.

References

Adult Learning Program. 2001. *Learn how the pros make 'em laugh*. Auburn, Mich.: The Humor Institute. (4 CD set.)

Alena Group. 2003. *Leadership and Humor*. www.alineagroup.com/Leaders%20 Humor.htm (accessed April 2, 2003).

Banning, M. R., and D. L. Nelson. 1987. The effects of activity-elicited humor and group structure on group cohesion and affective structure on group cohesion and affective responses. *American Journal of Occupational Therapy* 41, no. 8: 510–14.

Barecca, R. 1991. Laughing all the way to the bank: Humor and strategies for success. In *They used to call me snow white but I drifted: Women's strategic use of humor*. New York: Penguin.

Barlow, C., J. Blythe, and M. Edmonds. 1999. *A handbook of interactive exercises for groups*. Boston, Mass.: Allyn & Bacon.

Begley, S. 2000. The science of laughs. *Newsweek* 36, no. 15 (October 9): 75–76.

Bennis, W. 1959. Leadership theory and administrative behavior: The problem of authority. *Administrative Science Quarterly* 4:259–301.

Bennis, W., and B. Nanus. 1985. *Leaders: The strategies for taking charge*. New York: Harper & Row.

Berger, A. A. 1993. *An anatomy of humor*. New Brunswick, N.J.: Transaction Publishers.

Berk, R. A. 2000. Does humor in course tests reduce anxiety and improve performance? *College Teaching* 48, no. 4 (fall): 151–58. (ERIC No. EJ 619990)

Bolman, L. G., and T. E. Deal. 1997. *Reframing organizations: Artistry, choice, and leadership*. 2nd ed. San Francisco: Jossey-Bass.

Brooks, G. P. 1992. *Humor in leadership: State of the art in theory and practice.* (ERIC No. ED 417113)

Burford, C. T. 1985. The relationship of principals' sense of humor and job robustness to school environment. *Dissertation Abstracts International* 46, no. 10: 215. (UMI No. AAG 8516001)

Burger, M. Leadership and humor: Using humor as a tool for leadership. n.d. http://www.alineagroup.com/pdfs/Leadership%20and%20Humor.pdf (accessed March 9, 2004).

Burns, J. M. 1978. *Leadership.* New York: Harper and Row.

Chang, M., and C. R. Gruner. 1981. Audience reaction to self-disparaging humor. *Southern Speech Communication Journal* 46, no. 4: 419–26.

Coleman, J. G., Jr. 1992. All seriousness aside: The laughing-learning connection. *International Journal of Instructional Media* 19, no. 3: 269–76.

Crawford, C. B. 1994. Strategic humor in leadership: Practical suggestions for appropriate use. Paper presented at the meeting of the Kansas Leadership Forum, Salina, Kansas, May. (ERIC No. ED 369107)

Creguer, T. 1991. Dissertations of the weird and famous. *Research Update* 20 (fall). Ann Arbor, Mich.: University Microfiche International, 4–5.

Culberson, R. P. 2000. Humor at work. *Frankly Speaking Newsletter* 7, no. 4 (November–December). www.frankassociates.com/news/news7-4.html (accessed July 12, 2003).

Curtis, D. B., and T. L. Hansen. 1990. *Humor in the workplace: A communication tool. An annotated bibliography.* Annandale, Va.: Speech Communication Association. (ERIC No. ED 319085)

Davis, A., and B. H. Kleiner. 1989. The value of humour in effective leadership. *Leadership and Organizational Development Journal* 10, no. 1, i-iii.

Davis, J. M., and A. Farina. 1970. Humor appreciation as social communication. *Journal of Personality and Social Psychology* 15, no. 12: 175–78.

Desberg, P. 1981. The effect of humor on retention of lecture material. Paper presented at the annual meeting of the American Psychological Association. (ERIC No. ED 223118)

Dickmann, M. H., and N. Stanford-Blair. 2002. *Connecting leadership to the brain.* Thousand Oaks, Calif.: Corwin Press.

Dole, B. 2001. *Great presidential wit: Laughing (almost) all the way to the White House.* New York: Scribner.

Donnelly, D. 1992. Divine folly: Being religious and the exercise of humor. *Theology Today* 48, no.4 (January). http://theologytoday.ptsem.edu/jan1992/v48-4-article1.htm (accessed July 14, 2003).

Duncan, W. J. 1982. Humor in management: Prospects for administrative practice and research. *Academy of Management Review* 7, no. 1: 136–42.

———. 1984. Perceived humor and social network patterns in a sample of task-oriented groups: A reexamination of prior research. *Human Relations* 37:895–907.

Duncan, W. J., and J. P. Feisal. 1989. No laughing matter: Patterns of humor in the workplace. *Organizational Dynamics* 17:18–30.

Duncan, W. J., L. R. Smeltzer, L. R., and T. L. Leap. 1990. Humor and work: A review of theory and research. *Annual Review of the Journal of Management* 16, no. 2 (June): 255–78.

Eastmond, J. N., Jr. 1992. *Probing project humor for insights in ethnography: A case study* (November). (ERIC No. ED 353322)

Edwards, C. M., and E. R. Gibboney. 1992. *The power of humor in the college classroom.* (February). (ERIC No. ED 346535)

Fauber, J. 2000. Laughter may be best medicine. *Milwaukee Journal/Sentinel*, November 16, 2a.

Feingold, A., and R. Mazzella. 1991. Psychometric intelligence and verbal humor ability. *Personality & Individual Differences* 12, no. 5: 427–35.

Fiegelson, S. 1998. Energize your meetings with laughter. Alexandria, Va.: Association for Supervision and Curriculum Development.

Freud, S. 1905/1960. *Jokes and their relation to the unconscious.* Trans, J, Strachey, New York: Norton.

Fry, W. F. 1986. Humor, physiology, and the aging process. In *Humor and Aging*, ed. by L. Nahemow, K. McCluskey-Fawcett, and P. McGhee, 81–98. Orlando, Fla.: Academic Press.

Gardner, H. 1981. How the split brain gets a joke. *Psychology Today* (February): 74–78.

———. 1995. *Leading minds: An anatomy of leadership.* New York: Basic Books.

Gesell, I. 1997. *Playing along: 37 group learning activities borrowed from improvisational theater.* Duluth, Minn.: Whole Person Associates.

Glassman, E. 1991. The creativity factor: *Unlocking the potential of your team.* New York: Pfeiffer & Co.

Glueck, I. 2001. Why do we laugh? A multidimensional theory. *Dissertation Abstracts International* 63, no. 1: 557. (UMI No. AAT3039003)

Goldstein, J. H. 1976. Theoretical notes on humor. *Journal of Communication* 26, no. 3: 104–12.

Gruner, C. R. 1965. An experimental study of satire as persuasion. *Speech Monographs* 32:149–53.

———. 1970. The effect of humor in dull and interesting informative speeches. *Central States Speech Journal* 21:160–66.

———. 1978. *Understanding laughter: The workings of wit and humor.* Chicago, Ill.: Nelson-Hall.

———. 1985. Advice to the beginning speaker on using humor—what the research tells us. *Communication Education* 34, no. 2 (April): 142–47.

Gunning, B. L. 2001. The role that humor plays in shaping organizational culture. *Dissertation Abstracts International* 62, no. 12A: 354. (UMI No. AAI3036377)

Hauck, W. E., and J. W. Thomas. 1972. The relationship of humor to intelligence, creativity, and intentional and incidental learning. *Journal of Experimental Education* 40, no. 4 (summer): 52–55.

Howard, P. J. 2002. *The owner's manual for the brain.* 2nd ed. Atlanta, Ga.: Bard Press.

Hudson, G. 1979. The role of humor in John F. Kennedy's 1960 presidential campaign. *Dissertation Abstracts International* 40, no. 6A: 106. (UMI No. AAG 7926311)

Hughes, R. L., R. C. Ginnett, and G. R. Curphy. 1995. What is leadership? In *The leader's companion: Insights on leadership through the ages*, ed. by J. T. Wren, 39–43. New York: Free Press.

Kaplan, R. M., and G. C. Pascoe. 1977. Humorous lectures and humorous examples: Some effects upon comprehension and retention. *Journal of Educational Psychology* 69, no. 1: 61–65.

Kets de Vries, M. F. R. 1990. The organizational fool: Balancing a leader's hubris. *Human Relations* 43, no. 8: 751–70.

Korobkin, D. 1988. Humor in the classroom: Considerations and strategies. *College Teaching* 36, no. 4 (fall): 154–58.

Kushner, M. 1990. *The light touch: How to use humor for business success.* New York: Simon & Schuster.

Lane, W. 1993. Strategies for incorporating humor into the school climate. *Schools in the Middle* 2, no. 4 (summer): 36–38. (ERIC No. EJ 465267)

Lipman-Blumen, J. 1996. *The connective edge: Leading in an interdependent world.* San Francisco: Jossey-Bass.

Littleton, J. 1998. Learning to laugh and laughing to learn. *Montessori LIFE* 10, no. 4 (fall): 42–44.

Marken, D. J. 1999. An exploratory study of the ways principals use humor and perceive that humor contributes to their leadership. *Dissertation Abstracts International* 60, no. 9A: 263. (UMI No. AAI9944522)

Markiewicz, D. 1974. Effects of humor on persuasion. *Sociometry* 37:407–22.

Martin, D. M. 2001. Women, work, and humor: Negotiating paradoxes of organizational life. *Dissertation Abstracts International* 62, no. 5: 226. (UMI No. 3015977)

Marzano, R. 2003. *What works in schools: Translating research into action.* Alexandria, Va.: Association for Supervision and Curriculum Development.

Masten, A. S. 1983. Humor and creative thinking in stress-resistant children. *Dissertation Abstracts International* 43, no. 11B: 518. (UMI No. AAG 8308093)

Meyer, J. 1990. Ronald Reagan and humor: A politician's velvet weapon. *Communication Studies* 41, no. 1: 76–88.

Osif, B. A., and R. L. Harwood. 2000. Change: Challenges and coping, part II. *Library Administration & Management* 14, no. 1 (winter): 39–44. (ERIC No. EJ 611605)

Pease, R. A. 1991. Cartoon humor in nursing education. *Nursing Outlook* 39, no. 6 (December): 262–67.

Pollak, J. P., and P. D. Freda. 1997. Humor, learning, and socialization in middle level classrooms. *The Clearing House* 70, no. 4 (March–April): 176–78.

Popkin, R. H. n.d. *Encyclopedia of Philosophy.* www.roberthanan.com/heresy/pascal.html (accessed March 4, 2003).

Provine, R. 2000. *Laughter: A scientific investigation.* New York: Penguin Books.

Rareshide, S. W. 1993. *Implications for teachers' use of humor in the classroom.* (ERIC No. ED 359165)

Salkind, N. 2000. *Statistics for people who think they hate statistics.* Thousand Oaks, Calif.: Sage Publications.

Salovey, P., and D. Sluyter. 1997. *Emotional development and emotional intelligence: Educational implications.* New York: Basic Books.

Schlechty, P. 1998. *Creating a capacity for change: Philip Schlechty on the future of education.* Carlsbad, Calif.: CRM films.

Scriven, J., and L. Hefferin. 1998. Humor: The "witting" edge in business. *Business Education Forum* 52, no. 3 (February): 13–15.

Senge, P. M. 1990. *The fifth discipline: The art and practice of the learning organization.* New York: Currency Doubleday.

Senge, P. M., Ross R., Smith, B., Roberts, C., & Kleiner, A. (Eds.). 1994. *The fifth discipline fieldbook.* New York: Doubleday.

Seuss, Dr. 1956. *The cat in the hat.* New York: Random House.

Shammi, P., and D. T. Stuss. 1999. Humor appreciation: A role of the right frontal hole. *Brain* 122, no. 4 (April): 657–66.

Simons, G. 1997. The uses and abuses of humor in a multicultural world. *Managing Diversity Newsletter* (November): 1–3.

Sinha, D., and H. Misra. 1960. Qualities desirable for engineering students and profession: I. Teachers sample. *Journal of Psychological Researches* 5, no. 1: 10–22.

Sousa, D. 1995. *How the brain learns: A classroom teacher's guide.* Reston, Va.: National Association of Secondary Schools Principals.

Stevenson, D. 2002. The eight steps of story structure. *Story Theater Newsletter*, no. 3 (January): 1. http://www.storytheater.net/art.shtml# (accessed March 5, 2003).

Sutherland, J. C. 1982. The effect of humor on advertising credibility and recall. Paper presented at the annual meeting of the Association for Education in Journalism, July. (ERIC No. ED 218627)

Svebak, S. 1977. Some characteristics of resting respiration as predictors of laughter. In *It's a funny thing, humor*, ed. by A. J. Chapman and H. C. Foot. Oxford: Pergamon.

Taylor, P. M. 1974. An experimental study of humor and ethos. *Southern Speech Communication Journal* 39:359–66.

Thompson, J. L. 2000. Funny you should ask, what is the effect of humor on memory and metamemory? *Dissertation Abstracts International* 61, no. 8B (March): 88. (UMI No. AAI 9983671)

Tribble, M. K., Jr. 2001. Humor and mental effort in learning. *Dissertation Abstracts International* 62, no. 9A: 110. (UMI No. AAI 3025409)

Vega, G. M. 1990. *Humor competence: The fifth component.* (ERIC No. ED 324920)

Vinton, K. L. 1989. Humor in the workplace: It is more than telling jokes. *Small Group Behavior* 20, no. 2 (May): 151–66.

Visco, F. L. n.d. How to write good. home.europa.com/~walsup/Visco.html (accessed June 18, 2003).

Wallinger, L. M. 1997. Don't smile before Christmas: The role of humor in education. *NASSP Bulletin* 81, no. 589 (May): 27–34.

Walters, L. 1995. *What to say when . . . you're dying on the platform.* New York: McGraw-Hill.

Weinstein, M. 1986. *Lighten up: The power of humor at work.* Greenwich, Conn.: Listen USA (cassette recording).

Wheatley, M. J. 1994. *Leadership and the new science: Learning about organization from an orderly universe.* San Francisco, Calif.: Berrett-Koehler.

Winnick, C. 1976. The social contexts of humor. *Journal of Communication* 26, no. 3: 124–28.

Wuerffel, J., J. DeFrain, and N. Stinnett. 1990. How strong families use humor. *Family Perspective* 24, no. 2: 129–41.

Ziegler, V., G. Boardman, and M. D. Thomas. 1985. Humor, leadership, and school climate. *The Clearing House* 58, no. 8: 346–48.

Ziv, A. 1988a. Humor's role in married life. *International Journal of Humor Research* 1:223–29.

———. 1988b. Teaching and learning with humor: Experiment and replication. *Journal of Experimental Education* 57, no. 1: 5–15.

Zola, S. 2003. Ah yes, I remember it well . . . Remembering, Forgetting and the Movie "Memento." Irvine Health Foundation, The Lecture Series. www.ihf.org/lecture/zola_trans.html (accessed March 3, 2003).

Index

About the Author

Peter Jonas has been involved in higher education for more than twenty years, serving as a director of institutional research, assistant dean, and faculty member in the areas of research, leadership, and technology. Dr. Jonas has also been actively involved in consulting for the past fifteen years, and has made numerous presentations across the country on the topics of research (program evaluation), assessment, leadership, humor, and technology.